UNDER WHICH KING?

UNDER WHICH KING?

A Study of
The Scottish Waverley Novels

ROBERT C. GORDON

OLIVER & BOYD

EDINBURGH
LONDON

1969

OLIVER AND BOYD LTD

Tweeddale Court
Edinburgh 1

First published 1969

0 500163 26
Printed in Great Britain
By R. & R. Clark Ltd. Edinburgh
Scotland

CONTENTS

ABBREVIATED TITLES
OF WORKS OFTEN CITED IN FOOTNOTES

The Waverley Novels

These are cited by reference to the Dryburgh Edition, London 1892-5.

A.	=	*The Antiquary.*
B.D.	=	*The Black Dwarf.*
B.L.	=	*The Bride of Lammermoor.*
F.M.P.	=	*The Fair Maid of Perth.*
F.N.	=	*The Fortunes of Nigel.*
G.M.	=	*Guy Mannering.*
H.M.	=	*The Heart of Midlothian.*
L.M.	=	*The Legend of Montrose.*
O.M.	=	*Old Mortality.*
Q.D.	=	*Quentin Durward.*
R.	=	*Redgauntlet.*
R.R.	=	*Rob Roy.*
S.R.W.	=	*St Ronan's Well.*
W.	=	*Waverley.*

Other Works

Journal = *The Journal of Sir Walter Scott*, ed. J. G. Tait, 3 vols., Edinburgh 1939-46.

Letters = *The Letters of Sir Walter Scott*, ed. H. J. C. Grierson, 12 vols., London 1932-7.

Lockhart = JOHN GIBSON LOCKHART, *Memoirs of The Life of Sir Walter Scott*, 5 vols., Boston and New York 1901.

M.P.W. = *The Miscellaneous Prose Works of Sir Walter Scott, Bart.*, 28 vols., Edinburgh 1851-7.

PREFACE

I have attempted here, not to tell the whole truth about the Waverley Novels, but to give an appreciative account of those that relate to Scottish life from the mid-seventeenth to the early nineteenth centuries. In taking them up in chronological fashion I have adopted Scott's preference for straight-line narrative, but with a particular purpose in mind—the revelation that Scott's responses to the changes in Scottish life and manners that occurred during these crucial generations were not uniform, and that his Scottish novels exhibit a rough pattern of development from *Waverley* to *Redgauntlet*.

Some readers may be more impressed with the roughness than with the pattern. I hope they are. The enemy of well-intentioned Scott criticism is excessive tidiness, and the danger at the present time may be that the new and quickly burgeoning interest in Scott may produce an overabundance of conflicting dogmatic interpretations.

It would be misleading to claim absolute freedom from such tendencies. Permit me, therefore, to confess certain biases of my own, especially since some of them are unorthodox. The reader must understand that I present them solely for his information and with no polemical purpose.

First, I am not as concerned as some critics would wish about the integrity of the novel as a *genre*. A characteristic of the form as Scott knew it was its openness to invasion from other forms as well as its frequent imitation of those forms. *Tom Jones* is thus an epic, a biography, and a collection of essays. I am aware of the very sound reasons why others believe that the novel must be treated with the full aesthetic rigour bestowed, say, upon a sonnet by Gerard Manley Hopkins, but I think such rigour can be an impediment to an understanding of Scott. Scott, of course, was a good critic of fiction with a firm sense of relevance, and his novels often exhibit impressive formal qualities. Yet his extensive use of explanatory notes, to cite only one example, suggests a lack of anxiety about the ontological defences of his medium that I do not find disturbing.

Second, I enjoy " character-mongering "—the exploitation of individual eccentricities for their own sake. Scott was less inclined to this practice than some may think, but he was capable of it at times, and, again, I do not object.

Third, although the formal hero of a novel may fail to exhibit a significant moral growth, such failure does not strike me as disastrous to the novel.

Fourth, although I have chosen for the most part to discuss the Scottish novels as self-contained literary works, I admit that I would never have undertaken the task had I not felt in the novels the presence of a personality that I admire and like. It may be said, of course, that " The Author of Waverley ", not to mention such *personae* as Jedediah Cleishbotham and Peter Pattieson, is as much a literary creation as Caleb Balderstone, but I consider the difference between such figures and Scott himself to be negligible. My occasional use of Lockhart's or Scott's letters and *Journal* in part reflects this conviction.

Fifth, to confess a limitation, although my emphasis upon Scott's unusual handling of fathers and guardians may suggest Freudian concepts, I am not professionally competent to apply such concepts either to Scott or his characters. Hence, in discussing the father-son conflicts in the novels I have employed the same language usually applied to differences in temperament in ordinary circumstances.

R. C. G.

I

CONFLICTS
AND CONTRADICTIONS

"... from the first his dramatic sympathies array
themselves on the side which judgement condemns."

— Julia Wedgwood

Sir Walter Scott was a great novelist with a weak aesthetic
conscience. He never entirely escaped from a conviction that
writing was a scribbler's trade, unworthy of the landed gentleman or the man of business. The magnificence of his successes
was a virtue achieved by a powerful imagination working up-
stream against a current of doubt and prejudice that would have
defeated any lesser talent. He once praised Byron, in words that
chill, for achieving literary fame while " managing his pen with
the careless and negligent ease of a man of quality." [1] It was, in
its justification of literary Whiggery by an appeal to aristocratic
principle, a characteristic compliment.

Scott's environment offers abundant evidence that Scott's
environment and upbringing were largely responsible for his
dim view of his highest gifts. In Edinburgh, his native city, the
tradition of John Knox had been eclipsed, but not extinguished,
by the enlightenment of the eighteenth century, and although its

[1] *M.P.W.*, IV. 375.

enthusiasm was supposedly dead, it would not lie down. Its spirit, combined with humanistic rigour, undoubtedly contributed to that interesting list of topics for discussion proposed to the Edinburgh Belles Lettres Society shortly after its founding in 1759. Among the questions presented were the following:

Whether the present prevailing game of cards tends to corrupt the morals of young people?

Whether the conduct of the Romans in ravishing the Sabine women can be reconciled with the principles of honour and justice?

Should reading and writing of romances be discouraged? [2]

Scott, of course, rebelled against Calvinistic dogmatism and austerity and became an Episcopalian,[3] but the dreary sermons he heard as a child at the Old Greyfriars' church must have imprinted more than the memory of boredom. And there was always his father to drive the lessons home.

Scott's father was no Mr Barrett, and he was genuinely respected by his son. Still, it is difficult to feel very warmly toward him. There was more than a touch of the Philistine about the man, particularly in his view of imaginative literature as idle nonsense. Saunders Fairford of *Redgauntlet*, whom Scott patterned, with retrospective geniality, after his parent, has this to say of a young man he dislikes: " Unstable as water, he shall not excel. . . . He goeth to dancing-houses, and readeth novels—*sat est.*"[4] Lockhart, citing William Clerk, confirms the identity of Fairford and Scott's father. He also tells us that he so distrusted the pleasures of the table that he dashed cold water into

[2] Quoted by Harold William Thompson in *A Scottish Man of Feeling: Some Account of Henry Mackenzie, Esq., of Edinburgh and of the Golden Age of Burns and Scott*, London and New York 1931, pp. 62-3. For a good account of political and religious issues in eighteenth-century Scotland see David Daiches, *The Paradox of Scottish Culture: The Eighteenth-Century Experience*, London 1964.   [3] Lockhart, v. 456.

[4] *R.*, Letter 2. All references are to the Dryburgh Edition of the Waverley Novels, London 1892-5.

his plate of soup if its taste was too seductively good, and that he had a passion for funerals and took his son to as many as time allowed.[5] Such were the joys of life with the senior Scott.

There are times when the son imitates this man very well indeed—calling his own works " trifles," " rattles and ginger-bread," a " mere elegance, a luxury contrived for the amusement of polished life," " cursed lies." [6] And there is the advice he gave one of his young correspondents on the proper attitude toward a career in literature :

> I would caution you against an enthusiasm which, while
> it argues an excellent disposition and a feeling heart,
> requires to be watched and restrained, tho' not repressed.
> It is apt, if too much indulged, to engender a fastidious
> contempt for the ordinary business of the world, and
> gradually to unfit us for the exercise of the useful and
> domestic virtues. . . .[7]

But Scott, in truth, was not fundamentally submissive at all. He not only wrote poems and novels with gusto, he also developed an affectionate interest in writers of Cavalier temperament. Christina Keith was right to stress the importance of his edition of Dryden.[8] Concerning the language and situations of works like *Limberham* and *The Spanish Friar* Scott confronted the timid with downright defiance : "I will not castrate John Dryden. . . ."[9]

More interesting still is Scott's handling of the fathers and father-surrogates of his fictional heroes. They are a morally ambiguous group in which the good are decisively outnumbered by fools, timeservers, bigots, and bores. As we shall see, this muted but persistent revenge provides one of the most fascinating recurrent *motifs* in Scott's work. Scott was perfectly aware

---

[5] Lockhart, I. 65, 92-3, 166-7, 208-9 ; IV. 534.

[6] *Letters*, III. 481 ; *Journal*, ed. J. G. Tait, 3 vols., Edinburgh 1939-46, III. 59-60 ; *M.P.W.*, III. 108 ; *Journal*, II. 81.

[7] *Letters*, II. 278.

[8] *The Author of Waverley : A Study in the Personality of Sir Walter Scott*, London 1964, p. 79.   [9] *Letters*, I. 264.

that the narrative imagination is amoral. " My rogue," he once wrote, " always in despite of me, turns out my hero." [10] But his imagination had its own purposes, and one of these was to put Walter Scott senior in his place.

Scott also exhibited rebelliousness in other ways. He rebelled against literary rules, not only sterile and restrictive ones, but simpler common-sense disciplines. He had a gambler's impatience and a fatalistic distaste for significant revision. If a novel proved intractable he would send it out to the public regardless and then give the dice another toss. As he put it to James Ballantyne after the comparative failure of *The Monastery* : " If it is na weel bobbit we'll bobb it again." [11] His view of the literary world around him supported this practice. As Harry Levin puts it, Scott was " the last minstrel and the first bestseller." [12] Scott himself would have laughed at this description, for he could see his own success as indicating the decay of " minstrelsy." His was " the iron time." Once there had been the Elizabethan poetic dramatist, providing a vital literature for a society all of whose ranks were responsive to poetry. Now the popular novelist sat at his desk nourishing " that half-love of literature, which pervades all ranks in an advanced state of society." [13]

And his was " the iron time " in another sense. The age of Napoleon exalted the soldier and the loyalist, not the writer. Scott in his private discourse was a red-hot Tory, a man who could enjoy damning the Whigs with his frequently intolerant son-in-law, and who participated in Tory exaggerations to the extent of actually believing at one time that 50,000 Northumbrian " blackguards " were about to initiate a revolution. [14] The self-conscious aesthete, the man vain of his talent, the poetic senti-

[10] *Letters*, III. 220.   [11] *Letters*, VI. 160.
[12] *The Gates of Horn : A Study of Five French Realists*, New York 1963, p. 45.   [13] *M.P.W.*, III. 108.
[14] Henry Cockburn, *Memorials of His Time*, Edinburgh 1872, p. 366 n. See, in addition, Lockhart, III. 416 and the interesting comments of Francis R. Hart, " Proofreading Lockhart's *Scott* : The Dynamics of Biographical Reticence," *Studies in Bibliography*, XIV (1961), pp, 17-18.

mentalist—these human types were offensive luxuries in an age that demanded rougher virtues. Scott himself much enjoyed playing soldier, hacking away at targets in drills with the Edinburgh Light Horse, [15] or writing " in my old Cossack manner " for the benefit of " soldiers, sailors and young people of bold and active disposition." [16] Lockhart's designation of Scott as " the ' mighty minstrel ' of the Antigallican war " [17] has more than rhetorical significance.

Nevertheless, the man was nothing if not contradictory. The same writer who could endorse Lord Byron's " negligent ease " could also resent Horace Walpole's aristocratic dilettantism.[18] And with all his fondness for images of war and scenes of blood, with all his crisis Toryism and his readiness to dispatch grapeshot among the masses, he remained fascinated by pacifists and quietists of all sorts—the peaceful farmers who gave Edward Waverley time to realise that he was no warrior, the Dinmonts of *Guy Mannering*, Bessie Maclure of *Old Mortality*, Lucy Ashton of *The Bride of Lammermoor*, Joshua Geddes of *Redgauntlet*—all convinced of the vanity of arms, soldiership, and sometimes even of action itself. Scott, among other things, was an unusually peaceful man.

So contradictory a writer was bound to reveal his inner conflicts not only in his compositions but also in the way he composed. His *Journal*, where Scott is resolute in honest self-analysis, is full of rebellious utterances against order, method, and duty :

... propose to me to do one thing, and it is inconceivable the desire I have to do something else....

Having ended the Second Vol of *Woodstock* last night, I have to begin the Third this morning. Now I have not the slightest idea how the story is to be wound up to a catastrophe.... I never could lay down a plan—or, having laid it down, I never could adhere to it....

15 Lockhart, I. 240-1.
16 *Letters*, II. 170, and *Journal*, I. 186.
17 Lockhart, II. 42.   18 *M.P.W.*, III. 304.

I ought to correct them [the proofs of *Woodstock*].
Now, this *ought* sounds like as possible to *must*, and *must*
I cannot abide.

When I *convey* an incident or so, I am at as much pains
to avoid detection as if the offence could be indicted . . .
at the Old Bailey.

There must be two currents of ideas going in my mind
at the same time. . . .

The phrase *hoc age* often quoted by my father does
not jump with my humour. I cannot nail my mind to
one subject of contemplation, and it is by nourishing two
trains of ideas that I can bring one into order.[19]

Here, however, we must avoid confusing procedures with
results. Scott could write novels that do, indeed, suggest a kind
of ruminating improvisation. *The Antiquary* is an example.
But other works have strong cohesion and structural consis-
tency—*Waverley*, *Old Mortality*, *The Bride of Lammermoor*,
Quentin Durward, *The Fair Maid of Perth*. Mozart and Beethoven were masters of musical form. Mozart did much of his
work in his head ; Beethoven worked with sketchbooks, revising
and discarding constantly. The differences in method were
irrelevant. Scott's worst faults as a novelist resulted, not from
headlong work habits, but from a degree of contempt for his
craft and for his public that occasionally allowed commercial
considerations of a cheap sort to rule his imagination. And so
he produced the padded conclusion of *The Heart of Midlothian*,
the resurrection of Athelstane in *Ivanhoe*, the false and disastrous
conclusion of *St Ronan's Well*.

Scott has been scolded for such crimes. The problem
today is that his virtues are too often forgotten in the scolding.
These virtues include more than his renowned gift for Scots
dialect, his skill in humorous characterisation, his ability to
manage scenes of brute action. There are also the virtues
of a narrative style which, though vulnerable to easy ridicule

[19] *Journal*, I. 27 ; 100-1 ; 146 ; 249 ; II. 147 ; III. 21.

as " filleted Johnson," [20] conveys as few other styles have done the sensation of narrative as a delight in itself. This style, moreover, was that of an irrepressible mimic and story-teller for whom fiction could never have been vastly different from oral narrative,[21] whose most significant scholarly activities were directed toward the preservation of a popular oral literature, and whose legal activities exposed him to situations in which judgment depended upon oral testimony. It should also be remembered that Scott's own speech never lost its " Border burr." [22] It may be inevitable that those reared outside of Scotland will read Scott's narrative style, which sometimes resembles a Latinised advocate's prose, as merely an eccentric form of English. But they should not forget that the distinction between the speech of his Scottish characters and his own style as it sounded in his mind was not as sharp as the printed page might make it appear. His " filleted Johnson," in short, has backbone.

Scott's inclination toward the oral and the mimetic, however, appears with equal clarity in his lifelong indebtedness to the drama. From his early childhood, when he was moved to cry aloud at a performance of *As You Like It*,[23] until his late years, when he pathetically hoped that his " goblin drama " *The Doom of Devorgoil* would help to satisfy his creditors,[24] Scott had a passion for the theatre that directly influenced his fiction. His good friend Daniel Terry not only put some of his novels on the stage, he also entertained Scott by mimicking his personal mannerisms.[25] And Scott's reaction to a performance of a play based upon *Rob Roy* was enthusiastic enough to suggest that for a moment his imaginative effort in creating the character of Bailie Nicol Jarvie had achieved complete fulfilment.[26] Moreover, a play—even a dull one like Logan's *Runnamede*—could suggest a leading story line for a novel,[27] while the Elizabethan dramatists

---

[20] Patrick Cruttwell, " Walter Scott," in *From Blake to Byron, A Guide to English Literature*, ed. Boris Ford, 7 vols., London 1962, v. 109.

[21] Lockhart, I. pp. 76, 98.   [22] Lockhart, v. 260 n.

[23] Lockhart, I. 18.   [24] *Journal*, I. 80-1.   [25] Lockhart, II. 153.

[26] *Letters*, v. 362.

[27] Introduction to *Ivanhoe*.

provided one of Scott's chief linguistic resources for suggesting the speech patterns of former ages.[28]

It would be wrong to suggest that Scott's indebtedness to the drama had uniformly happy results. The consequences for *St Ronan's Well*, as we shall see later, were disastrous, and in his handling of eighteenth-century French, German, or Dutch characters Scott seems to be perpetuating theatrical stereotypes. Nevertheless, the theatre supplied Scott with models of scenic presentation, and his novels often reveal a remarkable scenic competence. E. M. Forster, no friendly critic, admired Scott's skill in introducing new characters.[29] This is a theatrical gift. Furthermore, Scott's mastery of the large, tense, focused episode could triumph at times over weaknesses of style. Joseph Warren Beach pointed out that the language of Jeanie Deans's trial scene in *The Heart of Midlothian* is excessively paternal and solicitous, but he could not deny the dramatic power of the scene itself.[30] In fact, Scott's mastery of scenic tempo and structure may be responsible for one of the ironies of literary history. The famous opera performance in Forster's *Where Angels Fear to Tread* depends for one of its comic effects upon the contrast between English reverence for a " classical " novel by Scott and a rather wayward performance of *Lucia di Lammermoor* by a provincial Italian company.[31] It will not subvert Forster's fine comedy to tell the simple truth : once all the pragmatic necessities of libretto construction have been conceded, Donizetti's renowned sextet merely matches Scott's original scenic power and invention in Chapter 33 of *The Bride of Lammermoor*.

In sum, there is more good theatre in Scott than in the theatre he knew. Nevertheless, his dramatic material is presented to the reader through a personal narrative sensibility which, even while dwelling on guilt and misery, preserves the virtue of a Chaucerian

---

[28] See E. M. W. Tillyard, " Scott's Linguistic Vagaries," *Essays : Literary and Educational*, London 1962, pp. 99-107.

[29] *Aspects of the Novel*, New York 1927, p. 55.

[30] *The Twentieth Century Novel : Studies in Technique*, New York 1932, p. 17.

[31] London 1905, ch. 6.

tolerance, poised and humane. This tolerance reflects one of the more benign paradoxes of Scott—that a writer often considered a regionalist was one of the last fictional voices of a genuinely cosmopolitan European humanism.

This final point cannot be overemphasized. The fiction of the eighteenth century was one of the last gestures of a fading Renaissance culture, and it was there that Scott found his models. He seems to have had a particularly warm affection for Le Sage. To be sitting on a sofa reading *Gil Blas*—that was to him a reasonable image of Paradise.[32] We might wish to object, of course, that *Gil Blas* is not a good model for novelists to emulate. The *picaresque* plot is loose, there is padding at the end, forcibly lengthening a story that had already been satisfactorily concluded, and the narrative style is rather general and watery (" un repas chez lui, c'est un menu," wrote one critic).[33] None the less *Gil Blas*, among other virtues, presents very well the world of European *picaresque* fiction—a world of many roads, many inns, many cities, where a certain scepticism is required, since vice so easily counterfeits virtue, and where the local deities are Jesus, supervising the humbler charities, and the Stoic philosophers. Thus Gil Blas's occasional fits of greed or arrogance can be seen against a tradition of Christian humanism that judges him.

So it is with Scott, but more richly than with Le Sage, because he had more of the past in his bones. In a famous criticism of *The Antiquary*, E. M. Forster berated Scott because he " scribbles away about Early Christians " while some of his characters are in danger of drowning.[34] Forster's point is understandable, and it fits in with that emphasis on purity of *genre* that has characterised theories of fiction for over a hundred years. Such an emphasis judges Scott to be impure, with his tendency to open the world of his novels to alien forms of writing such as history, memoir, or essay. Still, I confess that Scott's readiness to remember the early Christians while Edie Ochiltree and his companions face

[32] *M.P.W.*, III. 408.
[33] Albert Cherel, " De Télémaque à Candide," *Histoire de la littérature française*, 9 vols., Paris 1933, VI. 127.
[34] *Aspects of the Novel*, pp. 57-8.

B

the rising tide is delightful to me. All characters in Scott, high and low, live in an enlarged world of historical and geographical time and space. The background glows and recedes. Scott's reservoir of allusion, always available and always abundant, makes this possible. The resulting enhancement of the human image is one of the peripheral benefits of an " impure " view of fiction.

But is the richness of the background betrayed by triviality and disorder in the foreground—sham Gothicism, hand-me-down plotting, and above all, slovenly construction? The answer to this question is to be found in that dualism that we have traced in Scott's temperament. Scott obviously felt within himself a conflict between passion and necessity, and that conflict, the basis of all intelligent literature, he projected into his view of history. In this way he gave his novels an underlying unity and relevance that can give meaning to apparent triviality, preserving all the while the sense that narrative itself is a pleasurable activity. Caleb Balderstone in *The Bride of Lammermoor*, going to ridiculous lengths to gather food for his master's kitchen, may impress a reader as " comic relief " gone wild, but Scott knows that Caleb is performing a charade—a latter-day mockery of feudal practices that makes his position in history pathetically clear.[35]

There is in most of Scott's work this sense of a conflict between past and present, ancient lawlessness and established law, passionate nostalgia and historical fact. In fiction, no principle of organisation is superior to a rich and awesome dichotomy. No wonder, then, that when Scott turned novelist he chose as the subject of his first effort the Jacobite Rebellion of 1745.

[35] *B.L.*, ch. 12.

2

WAVERLEY

"...the contest between the loyalists and their
opponents can never be obsolete..."

— Coleridge

The incorporating Union that brought England and Scotland
under one government in 1707 was, paradoxically, both a typical
example of eighteenth-century political jobbery and a gesture of
political faith—a premature ratification of things hoped for, if
not seen.[1] It could only acquire validity when Scotland began
to profit as a partner in British commercial, political, and intellectual life. Otherwise Scotland risked becoming what Scott
sometimes feared it *would* become—" a very dangerous North
British neighbourhood." [2]

For a long time after the passage of the Union there were few
visible benefits to the Scots. They had, it seems, lost their
independence for nothing, and when in 1736 the Crown pardoned
the unpopular Captain Porteous of the Edinburgh City Guard,
a man whose unruly authoritarianism had made him a symbol of
London's oppression of Scotland, the Edinburgh mob rioted in
a mood of nationalistic defiance. What was needed to prevent
an endless recurrence of this sort of thing was precisely the

[1] W. Ferguson, " The Making of the Treaty of Union of 1707," *The
Scottish Historical Review*, XLIII (1964), pp. 89-110.

[2] *Journal*, I. 133.

development that seemed to take place after mid-century—a lively incursion of Scots into the higher places of English life and an intellectual renaissance in Edinburgh. When the time came for Benjamin Franklin to remark that Jonah had swallowed the whale, the Union was validated.[3]

Before this could happen, however, the Jacobites were to be heard from. In the eighteenth century Jacobitism existed in a halfway house between activist determination and nostalgic gesture. There were chiefs in Scotland who were prepared to die for the old cause, and there were Tories in London who squeezed oranges in a marked manner, or, if they were like Samuel Johnson on a later occasion, recommended Jacobitism to pretty girls.[4] Between these poles were varying degrees of resolution (and a large measure of total indifference); and when Prince Charles misread the evidence and brought an army into the field it soon became clear where the preponderance lay. Nostalgia was one thing, grapeshot quite another.

As David Daiches has indicated, Scott looked back upon Jacobitism with divided feelings.[5] He was perfectly well aware that Scotland's commitment to a mercantile, secular, British world was irrevocable, and that such a world had great advantages over that of the Stuarts and the Highland patriarchs. Yet he sympathised with the rebels as the possessors of virtues no longer fashionable—feudal loyalty, personal heroism, chivalric flamboyance—and it would be ridiculous to underestimate the force of this sympathy. Not long before *Waverley* appeared he wrote to a correspondent, with his customary distaste for punctuation marks:

> Seriously I am very glad I did not live in 1745 for
> though as a lawyer I could not have pleaded Charles's
> right and as a clergy man I could not have prayed for
> him yet as a soldier I would I am sure against the con-

---

[3] Quoted in *The Writings of Thomas Jefferson*, Library Edition, 20 vols., Washington, D.C. 1903–4, XVIII. 167.

[4] *Boswell's Life of Johnson*, London 1946, I. 288.

[5] "Scott's Achievement as a Novelist," *Nineteenth-Century Fiction*, VI (1951), pp. 84–5. (Reprinted in *Literary Essays*, Edinburgh 1965.)

viction of my better reason have fought for him even to
the bottom of the gallows.[6]

His " better reason " could properly judge his Jacobite impulses,
but it could never completely contain them, and the consequences
for the novel of this failure of containment were enormous.

After Maria Edgeworth had opened his eyes to the possibility
of serious fiction exploiting distinct national traits,[7] Scott drama-
tised his conflicting impulses in novels of Scottish history. The
result was a new fictional mode—one that has been with us ever
since. For wherever novelists present social and political conflicts—France against Russia, America against Europe, North
against South, modern Africa against tribal Africa—they are
followers of Scott.

Waverley, then, is one of the most distinguished innovations
in literary history. It is also a splendid work in its own right.
Scott found his solution to the problems of dealing with Jacobitism in the story of an immature, vain, yet fundamentally proper
young hero who becomes a warrior of Prince Charles through
the interaction of youthful folly and the sheer power of circumstance. The structure of the story, despite some manipulations intended to preserve a sense of Edward Waverley's fundamental innocence, is simple and shapely. The hero begins as
a loyal servant of George II, deviates into Jacobitism, is dis-
illusioned, and returns to peace and sanity.

Scott begins the novel dead slow. Edward is to be taken into
treason step by step, and every contributing cause is to be laid
bare. One of these causes is the character of his father. Sir
Richard Waverley is a political opportunist who deserts Toryism
for his own profit. He marries for advancement and later gives
his son to the boy's childless and thoroughly Tory uncle in hopes
of eventually snaring the family estate for himself. Ironically,
Edward benefits from his father's greed by gaining a new
" father " : but we must not forget that, in effect, Edward is an
abandoned child. Sir Richard, a minor Machiavelli seeking profit

---

[6] *Letters*, III. 302.
[7] See the " General Preface " in *Waverley*.

among the political factions of the day, is the first of Scott's
worthless fathers.[8]

Edward's days on his uncle's estate are lingered over, but the
effect of these early chapters is delightful. Scott's style is playful,
detached, and discursive. Sir Everard has Jacobite sympathies;
what, then, was he doing during the uprising of 1715 ? Here is
Scott's answer :

> At the period of the Hanoverian succession he had
> withdrawn from parliament, and his conduct, in the
> memorable year 1715, had not been altogether unsus-
> pected. There were reports of private musters of tenants
> and horses in Waverley-Chase by moonlight, and of cases
> of carbines and pistols purchased in Holland, and
> addressed to the Baronet, but intercepted by the vigilance
> of a riding officer of the excise, who was afterwards tossed
> in a blanket on a moonless night, by an association of
> stout yeomen, for his officiousness. Nay, it was even
> said, that at the arrest of Sir William Wyndham, the
> leader of the Tory party, a letter from Sir Everard was
> found in the pocket of his night-gown. But there was
> no overt act which an attainder could be founded on, and
> government, contented with suppressing the insurrection
> of 1715, felt it neither prudent nor safe to push their
> vengeance farther than against those unfortunate gentlemen
> who actually took up arms.[9]

This humorous indirection, with its persistent use of the passive
(and its triumphant detail of the nightgown !) may make some
readers restless, but it serves very well to illustrate a major
characteristic of Jacobitism—its tentative, ambiguous flirtation
with death, its half-comic existence in a world of fearful political
possibilities. The Jacobitism of Sir Edward and his retinue was
strong, but it stopped short of the gallows. When Edward left
the family as a soldier, he had imbibed some of the Jacobite
ideology from those who were by temperament or circumstance

[8] *W*., ch. 2.   [9] *W*., ch. 5.

unable to act—the ageing Sir Everard, his ancient sister Rachel, the harmless High Anglican tutor Pembroke. In the light of subsequent events the opening chapters, with their relaxed and affectionate presentation of these characters, appear deeply ironic, for we see that these early associates were in effect gently and persistently leading Edward toward a possible death by hanging.

When Edward leaves his uncle's estate as an officer, he begins a journey northward, and Scott brings him closer to the geographical centre of Jacobitism. Again the narrative manner is relaxed. There is an increase in excitement, but the tempo remains nearly the same. How could it be otherwise when the Baron of Bradwardine is brought forward? He is a Jacobite whose loyalty to the past is very much like Uncle Toby's hobby-horse—an amiable obsession that grows by devouring every topic in view. Such men require room, and the Baron is given all he needs :

> " It represents . . . the chosen crest of our family, a
> bear, as ye observe, and *rampant* ; because a good herald
> will depict every animal in its noblest posture, as a horse
> *salient*, a greyhound *currant*, and, as may be inferred, a
> ravenous animal *in actu ferociori*, or in a voracious,
> lacerating, and devouring posture. Now, sir, we hold this
> most honourable achievement by the wappen-brief, or
> concession of arms, of Frederick Red-beard, Emperor of
> Germany, to my predecessor, Godmund Bradwardine. . . ." [10]

The Baron, however, is an eccentric with a difference. He rides his hobby-horse on to the battlefield for the Pretender, even though he sees the height of his glory, not in combat, but in the ancient ceremony of pulling off the Prince's shoe after the victory at Prestonpans.[11] Moreover, it is through the Baron's efforts that Edward meets the MacIvors, and when he does, Edward's journey into another world is emotionally, at least, complete, for he becomes a friend of Fergus and falls in love with his sister Flora.

[10] *W.*, ch. 11.   [11] *W.*, ch. 50.

Fergus's character is stretched taut between two worlds—
that of the French aristocracy, where he was reared as the son of
an exiled rebel of 1715, and that of primitive Highland loyalties
and superstitions. In the end the Highlands will win, and he will
go down to his death nobly, but visited by strange rages and
ghostly visions.

His sister, on the other hand, represents Jacobitism with the
utmost purity and unity of spirit. Flora may well be the most
important character Scott ever drew. There is no question,
however, that she is a partial failure as a figure in a novel. She
is too stagy as she poses by a waterfall, harp in hand, and sings
bad verses about Scotland's lost glory.[12] And her dialogues with
her brother show Scott at his worst, trying with the clumsiness
of a schoolboy to imitate the language of Europeanised sophisticates :

> " A truce, dear Fergus! spare us those most tedious
> and insipid persons of all Arcadia. Do not, for Heaven's
> sake, bring down Coridon and Lindor upon us."
> " Nay, if you cannot relish *la houlette et le chalumeau*,
> have with you in heroic strains."
> " Dear Fergus, you have certainly partaken of the
> inspiration of Mac-Murrough's cup rather than of mine."
> " I disclaim it, *ma belle demoiselle. . . .*" [13]

The importance of Flora is certainly not to be found in
scenes like this, but in the intensity of her dedication to the
Pretender's cause. She is, in truth, a celibate for political ends :

> " For myself, from my infancy to this day, I have had
> but one wish—the restoration of my royal benefactors
> to their rightful throne. It is impossible to express to
> you the devotion of my feelings to this single subject ;
> and I will frankly confess, that it has so occupied my
> mind as to exclude every thought respecting what is
> called my settlement in life." [14]

In other words, Flora's grand passion is the Pretender and

[12] *W.*, ch. 22.   [13] *W.*, ch. 23.   [14] *W.*, ch. 27.

all he stands for. What is startling here is the thoroughness with which the power of Eros has been diverted into a political channel. This sense of energy transferrred is strongly reinforced by that very weakness in the handling of ordinary courtship for which Scott is famous—a weakness exemplified in Edward's hopelessly stilted addresses :

> " Nay, dear Flora, trifle with me no longer ; you
> cannot mistake the meaning of those feelings which I
> have almost involuntarily expressed ; and since I have
> broken the barrier of silence, let me profit by my
> audacity." [15]

The truth is that a personal erotic attachment is too gratuitous and isolated a feeling to interest Scott. It is an emotion without a referent in history—a passion in the abstract. Flora easily tosses young Edward aside, but when the Jacobites are defeated she indeed becomes a woman " disappointed in love." For such women fictional tradition endorses a convent overseas, and that is precisely where Flora goes. She thus illustrates an important truth about Scott—that he was the father of the political novel primarily because he was seriously concerned with the passional and psychological consequences of our group-identifications as they are affected by the processes of history. We are close to the strange world of Jacobite minstrelsy, where legitimist sentiment adopts the language of the love-lyric. In Scott those feelings usually associated with intense erotic attachment—passionate obsession, fear of loss, nostalgic wretchedness in the event of failure—are most intensely displayed in areas of regional or ideological commitment. It is as though his conventional young lovers had been drained of their blood in order to give vitality to a vast drama of social love and hate.

Edward's affection for the MacIvors and for the Baron and his family, his past upbringing among English Jacobites, the intrigues of interested Highlanders—these will contribute to his eventual decision to join the Pretender's army. The progression is gradual, carefully thought out, and ultimately convincing.

[15] *W.*, ch. 26.

Although the MacIvors do not make a completely committed
rebel out of him, by the time he leaves for Edinburgh to report
to the authorities and clear himself of the suspicion of supporting
the enemies of the State he is in no mood to regard his Highland
friends as traitors deserving the gallows. And his first experiences among the Scottish Lowlanders complete the process of
political transformation.

Edward's Lowland adventures illustrate Scott's mastery of
the ironies of social and regional conflict. Since Scott is capable
of introducing major themes in quiet ways, one of these ironies
may pass unnoticed. It lies in the fact that Edward, brought up
in England, travels into a Presbyterian country on a Sunday.[16]
At once, and without being aware of it, he becomes an object of
disapproval. This theme of the conflict of cultures, implicit in
much that has gone before, is here sharpened by Scott's emphasis
on Edward's danger. Later, however, Edward will be favourably
misunderstood when his care of a dying man, bestowed largely
as an act of " general philanthropy," will be seen by his Highland
allies as the protective action of a chieftain toward a follower.[17]
Such visions of the gulfs of ignorance separating different regions
achieve their greatest clarity in that late and bitter masterpiece
The Two Drovers. The awareness that human divisions can
operate as absolutes not to be overcome by cosmopolitan or
liberal attitudes was one of the most significant results of Scott's
understandable interest in all dichotomies. In Edward's difficulties among the Scots the chastening conclusion of E. M. Forster's
A Passage to India is unmistakably foreshadowed.

Further ironies await Edward in the village of Cairnvreckan,
where he stops for the services of a blacksmith. The smith's wife
is a prancing old termagant, who, having heard of the outbreak
of the rebellion, declares for the Pretender and sings " Charlie
is my Darling " for the principal purpose of bedevilling her
husband. Because this uninhibited lower-class parody of Flora
takes Edward's part so vigorously as a subject for a row, Edward
is soon under arrest. She brings matters to a head by hinting
broadly that her husband is not the sole master of her body. Her

---

[16] *W*., ch. 30.   [17] *W*., ch. 48.

words have an incidental interest in that they reveal Scott as less of a proto-Victorian than some critics have found him :

"Gae hame, gudewife," quoth the farmer aforesaid ;
"it wad better set you to be nursing the gudeman's
bairns than to be deaving us here."
"*His* bairns ?" retorted the Amazon, regarding her
husband with a grin of ineffable contempt—"*His* bairns!"

"O gin ye were dead, gudeman,
And a green turf on your head, gudeman!
Then I would ware my widowhood
Upon a ranting Highlandman." [18]

Her words bring a suppressed titter from the crowd, but for Edward the results are disastrous. He becomes suspected of rebellion precisely because this woman takes his part, and he shortly finds himself under inquisition for defending himself against mob action with a pistol.

His inquisitor is Major Melville—very loyal, and very stuffy. Since Edward is on the defensive, the exchange between them is stiff with the rhetoric of gentlemen discussing questions of honour. But the scene contains one of Scott's clearest insights into the dangers of half-realised political gestures, for among the items of evidence cited against Edward is his possession of poor Pembroke's long-winded High-Church tracts and a letter from the most explicitly traitorous of his correspondents—Aunt Rachel! Edward, confronted with the prospect of the gallows partly because of the automatically rebellious maunderings of an ineffectual tutor and a comical spinster, may well feel "alone, unfriended, and in a strange land." [19] His is the same ironic dilemma as that of many American liberals of the McCarthy era, damned because of their friendships with men whose rebelliousness seemed very alarming indeed, because it existed, not as action, but as gesture.

From the time of his arrest all that is necessary to turn the angry and desperate Edward into an actual rebel is his rescue

[18] *W.*, ch. 30.   [19] *W.*, ch. 31.

from the Government's hands, and this is soon accomplished.
What follows is a time of excited fulfilment before and after the
Jacobite victory at Prestonpans. Edward, now a Jacobite officer,
becomes a social lion. He also becomes rather appealingly vain
and silly. A sense of pleasant anticipation tinged with fear is
conveyed in the conversation between Fergus's follower Evan
Dhu and the Edinburgh widow Mrs Flockhart, who likes a
pretty uniform as much as Edward himself. The scene gains
charm from Scott's approximation of ballad rhythm :

> " But will ye fight wi' Sir John Cope, the morn,
> Ensign Maccombich ? " demanded Mrs. Flockhart of her
> guest.
> " Troth, I'se insure him, an he'll abide us, Mrs.
> Flockhart," replied the Gael.
> " And will ye face thae tearing chields, the dragoons,
> Ensign Maccombich ? " again inquired the landlady.
> " Claw for claw, as Conan said to Satan, Mrs. Flockhart,
> and the deevil tak the shortest nails."
> " And will the colonel venture on the bagganets himsell ? "
> " Ye may swear it, Mrs. Flockhart ; the very first man
> will he be, by Saint Phedar."
> " Merciful goodness! and if he's killed amang the red-
> coats! " exclaimed the soft-hearted widow.
> " Troth, if it should sae befall, Mrs. Flockhart, I ken
> ane that will no be living to weep for him. But we
> maun a' live the day, and have our dinner ; and there's
> Vich Ian Vohr has packed his *dorlach*, and Mr Waverley's
> wearied wi' majoring yonder afore the muckle pier-glass;
> and that grey auld stoor carle, the Baron o' Bradwardine,
> that shot young Ronald of Ballenkeiroch, he's coming
> down the close wi' that droghling coghling bailie body
> they ca' Macwhupple, just like the Laird o' Kittlegab's
> French cook, wi' his turnspit doggie trindling ahint him,
> and I am as hungry as a gled, my bonny dow; sae bid
> Kate set on the broo', and do ye put on your pinners, for
> ye ken Vich Ian Vohr winna sit down till ye be at the

head o' the table ;—and dinna forget the pint bottle o' brandy, my woman." [20]

After Prestonpans, of course, the Jacobites confront the reality of external hostility and internal dissension. The cause disintegrates before our eyes, and Edward must be separated from it. It is after a miserable little skirmish in the North of England that the lost Edward, sheltered by a family of peaceful Cumberland farmers, realises " that the romance of his life was ended, and that its real history had now commenced." [21]

What follows this climax of self-understanding is curious. Edward, having gone out on a very long limb, must be inched back to safety again. Scott moves him about considerably in order to lead him to the inevitable marriage with the domestic Rose Bradwardine. But an important agent of salvation is Colonel Talbot, a Loyalist officer whose life Edward had saved at Prestonpans. Talbot's attitude toward Edward is partly paternalistic, for he is older, wiser, and more powerful. Yet he is not another father-substitute like Sir Everard or, later, the Baron of Bradwardine. Edward and Talbot often speak as equals, as though they were the ambassadors of two hostile nations, and their relationship is founded upon a balance of indebtedness, for each has saved the other's life. This element of reciprocity quietly anticipates similar relationships in later novels —Morton and Evandale in *Old Mortality*, Halbert and Edward Glendinning in *The Monastery* and *The Abbot*, and, most obviously, Darsie Latimer and Alan Fairford in *Redgauntlet*. What Scott seems to be working towards is the separation of a character type—" the hero "—into two persons, just as Flora MacIvor and Rose Bradwardine are symbolically divergent images of " the heroine." To do this, of course, is to carry dualism about as far as it will go. This is one more reason why a monistic view of Scott—that he was " really " a sentimental feudalist, or that he was " really " a rational son of the Enlightenment— can never be more than a half-truth.

The final chapters of *Waverley* deserve full attention, not only because of their merits as literature, but also because they offer an interesting compromise for Edward. First, however, the fates of the most active Jacobites must be made clear, and Scott, with an admirable sense of the relevant, barely mentions Culloden. What interests him, apart from the dilemma of his hero, is the destiny of the leading Jacobites—Fergus, Flora, and the Baron. The emotions aroused are elegiac and sometimes tragic, and they are intense. E. M. W. Tillyard has warned us all against the hand-me-down opinion that Scott lacks passion;[22] and he has ample support in these last scenes. Bradwardine's reception of Edward's appeal for permission to marry his daughter is an example :

> The Baron seemed collecting all his dignity to make a suitable reply to what, at another time, he would have treated as the propounding a treaty of alliance between the houses of Bradwardine and Waverley. But his efforts were in vain; the father was too mighty for the Baron; the pride of birth and rank were swept away; in the joyful surprise, a slight convulsion passed rapidly over his features, as he gave way to the feelings of nature, threw his arms around Waverley's neck, and sobbed out—" My son, my son! if I had been to search the world, I would have made my choice here." [23]

The intensity of this moment seems all the more marked when we consider Edward's previous observation that his real parent " never showed the affection of a father while he lived." [24] We may also remember Scott's identification of Edward with himself in his General Preface. Surely the abandoned Edward's quest for a father was a response to urgings from the depths of Scott's personality.

But Scott reserves his finest writing for the trial and execution of Fergus. The final judgment on the Laird of Glennaquoich by Edward's servant Alick Polworth is superb by any conceivable standard :

[22] *The Epic Strain in the English Novel*, London 1958, p. 69.
[23] *W.*, ch. 67.   [24] *W.*, ch. 61.

The next morning ere day-light he [Edward] took leave
of the town of Carlisle, promising to himself never again
to enter its walls. He dared hardly look back towards the
Gothic battlements of the fortified gate under which he
passed, for the place is surrounded with an old wall.
" They're no there," said Alick Polworth, who guessed
the cause of the dubious look which Waverley cast backward, and who, with the vulgar appetite for the horrible,
was master of each detail of the butchery,—" The heads
are ower the Scotch yate, as they ca' it. It's a great pity
of Evan Dhu, who was a very weel-meaning, good-
natured man, to be a Hielandman ; and indeed so was the
Laird o' Glennaquoich too, for that matter, when he wasna
in ane o' his tirrivies." 25

Some of Scott's admiring critics, who often seem to assume that
their readers are familiar with his every paragraph, quote Alick's
words in isolation. This is fatal, for the words require their
context. My inclusion of the entire paragraph is little better,
however, for the context really begins with the first chapter.
Alick is offering an apolitical Sancho's comment on the follies of
the great. Samuel Johnson insisted that " When a butcher tells
you that *his heart bleeds for his country*, he has, in fact, no uneasy
feeling." 26 Political excitement, in other words, is an upper-
class privilege. To a large extent Scott agreed, but the use he
made of the idea would have surprised Johnson. For what Scott
often finds among his low characters is an enviable and imperti-
nent indifference to the high-principled idiocies of the Ferguses
and Floras. After Scott's solemn account of the trial and execution of Fergus, Alick's words cut like a knife. We can almost
imagine him, his judgment delivered, spitting on the ground and
going forward with his saner business.

Still, Scott is not Alick. History in the grand sense, with its
impossible alternatives, existed for him. Flora's utopian fantasy
of an organic, independent society meant something—it pressed
hard upon his mind :

25 *W*., ch. 69.   26 Boswell's *Life*, I. 263.

" But let us hope a brighter day is approaching, when a Scottish country gentleman may be a scholar without the pedantry of our friend the Baron, a sportsman without the low habits of Mr Falconer, a judicious improver of his property without becoming a boorish two-legged steer like Killancureit." [27]

In the light of this vision of wholeness, we observe something unusual about Scott's conclusion. Edward returns to sanity after his bout of high adventure, but he does not come full circle. The truth is that Edward's renunciation of " the romance of his life " does not quite mean what it says, for it is softened at the end by Scott's desire that it should not be too absolute. Isn't there some safe compromise? There is. Edward not only marries the Baron's daughter, he also marries his estate, where he may breathe the air of the Highlands and participate in a life that preserves feudal virtues and pleasures without the physical and moral perils of feudal violence. Before the novel concludes, he has already begun to tell " tales of old Scottish manners " for the amusement of his friends, and the dead Fergus MacIvor lives on in an elegant oil-painting by " an eminent London artist." [28] Edward's settling into such a world prefigures Abbotsford.

All this seems a little suburban, and that is exactly the problem. Edward's fate did not really satisfy Scott. He had yet to exorcise the backward devils.

But if *Waverley's* compromise conclusion is not completely satisfying, this makes little difference to our evaluation of the novel as a whole. The reputation of *Waverley* has suffered far too much from its being the first of a long line. This position was actually an advantage, for the novel was a *début*, written under a sense of occasion and before Scott discovered what he could get away with in front of an adoring public. Its theme, moreover, is serious and new, its presentation of the ironies of history is precise and subtle, its structure shapely and well-ordered. There are some weaknesses in the presentation of Fergus and Flora, but there is not, with the exception of a stagy burlesque of a French

[27] *W.*, ch. 23.   [28] *W.*, ch. 71.

officer,[29] a cheap or opportunistic note from beginning to end. And Edward remains one of Scott's most engaging heroes—a young man who understandably finds the real world not to his taste, but whose confrontation with "romance" is something that his nature cannot support. These virtues, along with hundreds of lesser delights, offer reasonable grounds for considering *Waverley* Scott's finest novel. Certainly it must be ranked as high as any of the others.

[29] *W.*, ch. 58.

3

GUY MANNERING
&
THE ANTIQUARY

" The deil's in you, Monkbarns, for garring odds
and evens meet. Wha thought ye wad hae laid
that and that thegither ? "

— Edie Ochiltree to Jonathan Oldbuck

In the two novels that follow *Waverley* Scott narrows his scope.
Instead of national convulsions involving the armies of kings
and rebels we witness the struggles of smugglers, sheriffs, gipsies,
lawyers, and petty confidence-men. As is usual in Scott, the
relationship between past and present is an important theme, and
in this respect *Guy Mannering* and *The Antiquary* tell the same
tale as *Waverley*. There is, however, an interesting difference.
History's decision on the Jacobites was public and immutable,
but in the relatively isolated areas of Scotland where the two later
novels are set, Scott's conservatism had its way and the forces of
the past enjoyed some measure of success.

In *Guy Mannering* ancient virtue triumphs over modern
rascality in a way that makes this work morally less complex than
either *Waverley* or *The Antiquary*. Whereas *Waverley* depicts
the inevitable defeat of the principle of legitimacy strictly con-

strued, *Guy Mannering* elevates the same principle into a moral barrier between sheep and goats. The question at issue is the preservation of the Ellangowan estate as a patrimonial inheritance. Those who favour continuance are meant to receive our sympathy; those who do not are villains. Chief among the latter is Gilbert Glossin, a reprehensible " man of business " who enjoys none of that lawless tolerance that Scott often bestows upon his rogues. He cheats his way into the estate and then tries to eliminate the rightful heir. He is a scoundrel cut to the measure of Tory prejudice—an upstart, a man of cunning, not action, with no feeling for antiquity and no dignity. Everyone in the novel whose moral indignation is stirred by his graceless contempt for ancient privilege works against him.

The struggle for Ellangowan dominates the novel, but there are complications. Scott points out in his introduction that his first three or four chapters are the vestigial remains of what was intended as a tale of astrology, sin, and religious agony. He abandoned the idea because " astrology . . . does not now retain influence over the general mind sufficient even to constitute the mainspring of a romance." True enough, perhaps, but he kept his early chapters, nevertheless, and allowed the crises in the life of his hero, Harry Bertram, to follow the pattern predicted in Guy Mannering's horoscope. Moreover, he actually reinforced the element of prophecy by giving to Meg Merrilies, the gipsy who is chief among Bertram's supporters in his struggle for the estate, an independent capacity to foretell the time, place, and outcome of critical episodes. Such an over-supply of clairvoyance seems comically out of key with Scott's introductory rejection of astrology. What Scott was really rejecting, I suspect, was the necessity of dealing with astrology as a complex study with its own bristling " scientific " jargon. I also doubt whether the theme of religious struggle appealed to him when it involved an individual soul rather than ideological divisions within a society.

It could be argued that Scott's decision to retain his early chapters despite his change of plan was wise simply because of their excellence. The first chapter in particular is one of his masterpieces. It begins with a man on horseback in a darkening landscape, a subject perfectly suited to Scott's ambulatory style :

> It was in the beginning of the month of November
> 17— when a young English gentleman, who had just left
> the university of Oxford, made use of the liberty afforded
> him to visit some parts of the north of England ; and
> curiosity extended his tour into the adjacent frontier of
> the sister country. He had visited, on the day that opens
> our history, some monastic ruins in the county of Dumfries,
> and spent much of the day in making drawings of them
> from different points, so that, on mounting his horse to
> resume his journey, the brief and gloomy twilight of the
> season had already commenced.[1]

Despite the solecism in the last sentence, this passage, along
with its excellent companion piece in *A Legend of Montrose*, was
to become one of the most influential of beginnings. It foreshadows G. P. R. James's dogged imitations, as well as far more
impressive examples such as the opening of *The Return of the
Native* and *The Mayor of Casterbridge*. Moreover, it well
illustrates a particular virtue of Scott's style— its perfect appropriateness to a narrative role. It may be true that Scott's diction
and rhythms sometimes suggest Johnson, but he is not trying
to be like Johnson. Everything he writes, including his manuscripts, with their seamless, forward-slanting lines, suggests that
for Scott an English sentence was not an ordered spatial entity at
all, but a barely separable unit of narrative energy. Thus he
begins *Guy Mannering* with a time-indication, of all devices
perhaps the most seductive of attention, and continues with word
units that lead us on with a gentle but persistent pressure : " who
had just left the university of Oxford," " curiosity extended his
tour," " He had visited . . . and spent much of the day," " the
brief and gloomy twilight of the season had already commenced."
When reading Scott we must accept the principle that narrative
style is a prose *genre* unlike any other, and that its requisite
characteristics are movement, and the sense that every human

[1] *G.M.*, ch. 1.

action is a tentative reaching-out towards an obscure future. By such a definition Scott is a master.

The rider in the darkness is Guy Mannering, and he is soon in need of directions. We discover that the dangers he may be facing are increased by his being an outsider in Scotland. To make this clear Scott does something unusual for him—he thickens the Scottish dialect of the woman in the lonely hut whom Mannering consults : " Ye maun haud wessel by the end o' the loan, and take tent o' the jaw-hole." [2] This sort of thing is not common in the Waverley Novels. In fact, one of the most engaging characteristics of his nationalism is its diffidence. His Scottish dialect is usually so leavened with English phrases and rhythms that the definition of Scots words by means of their context is quite within the compass of an intelligent reader. His method here provides a parallel, within the British area, of his persistent deference to an existing catholic and European culture. But at the beginning of *Guy Mannering* he felt for the moment the pressure of that concern over the conflict of cultures which existed uneasily alongside his European humanism : thus he suggests that Mannering's linguistic ignorance could be as potentially troublesome as Edward Waverley's ignorance of the ways of a Scottish Sabbath.

Eventually, however, Mannering is received at the Ellangowan estate and given shelter as a benighted wanderer. Before long he casts a horoscope for the heir of Godfrey Bertram, who is born that night. Then he goes on his way, and with his departure Scott gets down to business on a subject that interested him far more than astrology—the conflict between antiquity and modernity. Dominating that conflict are Meg Merrilies and Gilbert Glossin. Meg is a gipsy whose loyalty to the Ellangowan inheritance is based upon a full awareness of tradition and mutual obligation. In one sense she, too, has an " estate," for she is a member of a cohesive race with its own inherited values, and her people have had extra-legal rights to occupy Ellangowan land for generations.[3] She also remembers with gratitude the alms she and her people have received.[4] She is a vessel of Burkian feeling,

---

[2] *Ibid.*   [3] *G.M.*, ch. 3.   [4] *G.M.*, ch. 28.

respecting the past and its " just prejudices," illustrating Scott's view of the world of inherited custom as a realm of grace where unforced charity is possible. She is also, like Flora MacIvor, the bearer of a utopian vision of a world both organically unified and heroic :

> " The times are sair altered since I was a kinchen-mort.
> Men were men then, and fought other in the open field,
> and there was nae milling in the darkmans. And the
> gentry had kind hearts, and would have given baith lap
> and pannel to ony puir gipsy. . . ." [4a]

There is, of course, a catch in this nostalgic rhapsody. It is delivered in the cant of criminals and includes a vision of violence that contrasts strangely with the picture of a kind-hearted gentry. Eventually Meg Merrilies will have to pay even more dearly than Flora for this streak of blood in the past she represents. In his view of history Scott was a pessimist, in so far as he found one element constantly present in all ages—sheer pugnacity. The antiquity that Meg recalls, when men " fought other in the open field," was perhaps psychologically more rewarding than the present, in that it imposed fewer hindrances between the urge to combat and its fulfilment. The modern world, by contrast, went to law, but at the cost, perhaps, of some emotional frustration. (Young Bertram's friend Dandie Dinmont, the Liddesdale farmer who is quarrelling with his neighbour over a postage-stamp of land, says, " We wad just take the auld gate [meaning broadswords] as readily, if it werena for the law.") [5] But the combative impulse persisted. There is no question, of course, that Scott always implies endorsement of the triumph of established law. By one means or another, the Ferguses, the Floras, and the Megs must be cast off. Still, Paulus Pleydell, that commendable lawyer who becomes almost as effective as Meg in restoring Ellangowan to its true heir, gives Dinmont a strange answer when he asks him to accept his case :

> " Confound you, why don't you take good cudgels and
> settle it ? "

[4a] *G.M.*, ch. 28:   [5] *G.M.*, ch. 38.

" Odd, sir," answered the farmer, " we tried that three times already. . . . But I dinna ken ; we're baith gey good at single-stick, and it couldna weel be judged."

" Then take broadswords, and be d--d to you, as your fathers did before you," said the counsel learned in the law.[6]

Thus the essentially altruistic Meg longs for a world of charity and honest bloodshed, Dinmont uses the law as a substitute for cudgelling, and the civilised Pleydell for a moment urges private war. Fortunately for the Waverley Novels, Scott was both stimulated and disturbed by the pressure of such contradictions as these.

Among the characters who share Meg's loyalty to the Bertrams, Pleydell, Mannering, and Dinmont are the most important. The young Bertram himself is primarily a counter whose position at the end of the game indicates the victor. Scott hardly bothers to present him directly as the lover of Julia Mannering, which is perhaps fortunate, but he commits an error in giving too much time to a misunderstanding between him and Mannering over past disagreements when both were on military service in India. Several chapters are devoted to creating the impression that a clash of high passions is imminent, but the clash never occurs, being swallowed up in the battle with Glossin.

Other characters are defined and judged in terms of this conflict. Godfrey Bertram, whose employment of Glossin furthers the ruin of an already diminished inheritance, is the second of Scott's contemptible fathers. He is almost oafish enough to be below any kind of moral evaluation, and as such he is rather well characterised by Scott, who enjoyed depicting stupid men. But his stupidity does not excuse his decision to drive the gipsies off the Ellangowan property.[7] Scott implies that this is an unnecessary breach of tradition, as well as a violation of the principle that a just society offers a certain charitable licence to ne'er-do-wells. When Bertram expels them, fate turns against him. Not only is his son abducted by smugglers,[8] but his career

[6] *G.M.*, ch. 36.   [7] *G.M.*, ch. 8.   [8] *G.M.*, ch. 9.

of mismanagement drives on to the point where he himself is expelled from his own land.⁹

The senior Bertram, then, is a man who proves unworthy of his inheritance. At the opposite extreme from this betrayal of the past is the folly of Sir Robert Hazlewood, a local magistrate who is of little use in the defence of the Ellangowan estate precisely because he takes his inherited position too seriously. He is " presumptuously over-conceited on the score of family pride and importance," and hates all the Bertrams of Ellangowan " because a certain baron of that house was traditionally reported to have caused the founder of the Hazlewood family hold his stirrup until he mounted into his saddle." Out of sheer snobbery he becomes a tool of Glossin's plot to guarantee that the hero never returns to claim his inheritance.¹⁰ Convinced that his theoretical knowledge of the law must never be sullied by the sort of practical application that smacks of real work, he can offer no effective legal resistance to the villain's activities. To Godfrey Bertram the past is only a faint trace in an opaque mind, to Sir Robert it is an ever-present excuse for useless pomposity. Neither of these men is of service in the effort to preserve its values.

Even persons of less practical relevance than these have meaning in the war between old and new. Ineffectuality is the essence of Mannering's tutor and companion Dominie Sampson, Scott's bookish footnote to Smollett's Lismahago. Sampson has an extensive but pedantic knowledge of the past; he is a counterpart of Meg, whose knowledge is narrow but completely experiential. Scott could not resist the temptation to bring them together for one discordantly funny scene. For him the confrontation between an antiquarian and a living fragment of antiquity was always rich in comic possibilities. Yeats asked of his classical scholars,

> Oh Lord, what would they say
> Did their Catullus walk that way ? ¹¹

---

⁹ *G.M.*, ch. 13.   ¹⁰ *G.M.*, ch. 42.
¹¹ *The Collected Poems of W. B. Yeats*, New York, 1951, p. 139.

Scott would not only have enjoyed Yeats's poem, he would also have been happy to supply the ensuing dialogue. When Sampson and Meg meet in a lonely place the Dominie spews out the Latin exorcisms he has learned from his reading :

" *Conjuro . . . abjuro, contestor atque viriliter impero tibi !* "

Meg is puzzled. She represents a world of primitive superstition in so absolute a fashion that the Dominie's words mean nothing to her. Hence the irony of her answer :

" What, in the name of Sathan, are ye feared for, wi' your French gibberish, that would make a dog sick ? " [12]

But antiquity in Scott must none the less abide a modern judgment, and its constant association with violence hovers over its representatives like a cloud of guilt. Meg may be a great force for good, but her earlier acquaintance with obsolete outlaws like the vicious Dirk Hatteraick must be atoned for by her death. The conclusion of *Waverley* shows us that for Scott a happy ending was one in which the hero settled into a historian's utopia where the ways of the past were preserved without the old accompaniment of violence. Meg, by her death, is both agent and victim of a similar purification, and the young Bertram will live in contentment because of it.

Guy Mannering does not really represent Scott at his best. Too much of his narrative energy is poured into the Bertram-Mannering story. The use of the epistolary method to keep the reader abreast of this story produces some charming letters from Julia Mannering to her shadowy correspondent, but there is an excess of them. Even Meg, with her passion for climbing on top of mounds of earth and declaiming as Scott thought Mrs Siddons might have done, forces too much contrived parallelism into her frequently lengthy speeches.[13] Her real talent lies in the direction of pungent brevity :

" The flints are gude," she said, " and the powder dry ; I ken this wark weel."

[12] *G.M.*, ch. 46. [13] *G.M.*, ch. 8.

" Dead ! ... dead ! that quits a' scores."

" He's a bonny corpse ... and weel worth the streaking."

" Aweel, eat your fill ; but an ye kenn'd how it was gotten ye maybe wadna like it sae weel."

" That was not spoken like a bairn of Ellangowan. ... It is the ill-doers are ill-dreaders."

She paused an instant beneath the tall rock where he had witnessed the burial of a dead body and stamped upon the ground, which, notwithstanding all the care that had been taken, showed vestiges of having been recently moved. " Here rests ane," she said ; " he'll maybe hae neibours sune." [14]

There remains, moreover, the vexing problem of the reader's opinion of Glossin. This opinion may not accord with Scott's intentions. No doubt of it—Glossin is a scoundrel of the worst sort. Nothing good can be said of the man, except perhaps that his conscience sometimes leads to a fighting in his soul. (Scott bestows nearly as much psychological description on Glossin as he gave to Edward Waverley.) Still, we hear too much of his being an upstart. When he enters Hazlewood's house, " The visitor, who had no internal consciousness of worth to balance that of meanness of birth, felt his inferiority...." Moreover, " he could not but be sensible that he was excluded from the society of the gentry of the county, to whose rank he conceived he had raised himself. He was not admitted to their clubs. ..." [15] Glossin is trying to make head against village Toryism, and I confess to some sympathy for him.

The best things in *Guy Mannering* appear as items of social history—the superb domestic and hunting scenes with the Dinmonts in Liddesdale,[16] Pleydell's " high jinks " in Edinburgh, a charming and utopian vision of neo-classical antics among Edinburgh lawyers that nicely balances the ridiculous picture of

[14] See, in succession, *G.M.*, chs. 53, 22, 27, 46, 53, and 53.
[15] *G.M.*, chs. 32 and 42. [16] *G.M.*, chs. 24-26.

the Roman banquet that Smollett put into *Peregrine Pickle*.[17] Finally, there is Scott's use of the Ellangowan setting—the " grey old towers of the ruin " and the woods that " advanced far into the ocean, waving in the moonlight along ground of an undulating and varied form." [18] It is a significant setting, returning throughout the novel as an ironically beautiful background to its deeds of violence. Moreover, something very similar to it, though far more stark and forbidding, is to reappear in *The Bride of Lammermoor*, where a family and its inheritance are, with tragic consequences, again at issue.

If *Guy Mannering* suffers from some weaknesses of structure, *The Antiquary* comes close to having no structure whatever. In his introduction Scott confesses his failure to create " an artificial and combined " narrative, but the narrative itself conveys no sense of guilt. Once more we have a missing heir whose return to his lands must be accomplished by the final chapter. An indication of Scott's casual utilitarianism in his handling of his hero occurs in Ch. 21, before the book is half over, when Lovel, having fought a duel and wounded his opponent, must take ship to avoid the law. He simply drops out of things until the conclusion brings him back. For half its length *The Antiquary* is " a novel without a hero."

Scott, however, made one emphatic change in the hero's story. Lovel's father is neither a low opportunist like Sir Richard Waverley nor a fool like Godfrey Bertram. Scott makes him the victim in a pageant of high aristocratic guilt and vengeance that comes parading on to the scene like a funeral procession at a school outing. Lovel's father, Lord Glenallan, is a Catholic penitent who has lived for years in the conviction, implanted by his vicious and strong-willed mother, that the marriage that produced his son was incestuous. Wasted by years of self-mortification, he dies wearing a hair shirt, even though the marriage is at last proved to have been innocent. Scott writes of him in the lurid fashion with which Protestant Gothicists of his time dealt with the darker aspects of Catholicism. He is certainly not a worthless man, but he *is* misguided, doomed,

[17] *G.M.*, ch. 36.   [18] *G.M.*, ch. 3.

miserable, and, in most of his appearances, unpleasant. With Glenallan the pattern of fatherhood changes, but by no means more favourably.

The Glenallan story is flamboyant, but the characters involved in it are not without interest. The old servant and *confidante* Elspeth Mucklebackit bears her own burden of guilt for aiding in the deception that turned Glenallan into a morbid penitent. Like Meg she is a fragment of the past atoning for the sins of the past, and her remarks offer a strange view of the traditional feudal virtues. Her comment on the ancient world of intense feudal loyalty is almost a parody of social nostalgia: "Nae man parted frae his chief for love of gold or of gain, . . ." she says, as though promising a sentimental look backwards. But the sentence continues, ". . . or of right or of wrang." [19] The amoral possibilities of the time-honoured virtue of loyalty contributed to the tragedy of Glenallan, for Elspeth, as a servant of Glenallan's mother, assisted in the deception of her son. In addition, the ancient clannish delight in keeping grudges warm, working together with the same national and cultural bias that got Edward Waverley into trouble, was one of her motives for hating Glenallan's bride. This innocent girl was English, and at one time she thoughtlessly mocked Scottish ways to Elspeth. "Yes, she scorned and jested at me," says Elspeth, "but let them that scorn the tartan fear the dirk!" [20]

The Glenallan tragedy is not the only plot element in *The Antiquary*. The other concerns a dishonest "adept" named Dousterswivel who swindles Sir Arthur Wardour with promises of easy wealth to be acquired through copper mining. The Dousterswivel episodes are easily the worst things Scott had yet devised. They are a running parody of fake supernaturalism that is bad in the flattest sort of way, lacking even the quaint extravagance of faded Gothicism.

Luckily *The Antiquary* has more to offer than the miseries of the Glenallans and the nonsense of Dousterswivel. There is Edie Ochiltree, the traditional licensed beggar who acts as a walking journal and almanac for the whole community of

[19] *A.* ch., 33.   [20] *Ibid.*

Fairport. If Elspeth is like Meg in her need to atone for a criminal past, Edie is like Meg in his ability to appear helpfully on the scene at critical moments. Scott's villages are like Fenimore Cooper's American wilderness in one respect—they need someone who gets about quickly, who can read signs in the wind, who can be relied on to deliver messages at crucial moments. Both Meg and Edie are in this respect like skilful frontiersmen. On the other hand, they are of help because tradition made them so, binding them to one place by the alms they have received and thus enabling them to become masters of the practical arts within a small area. The past may have had its bloody and deceitful side, but it also exhibited charity and a sort of psychological support for useful eccentrics. At the end of the novel Edie is still very much alive, but Elspeth, in accordance with Scott's pattern, dies in misery.

The main unifying element in *The Antiquary*, however, is Jonathan Oldbuck. He is Scott's most fully and extensively developed character so far—an amiable penny-pincher who combines the pedantry of Dominie Sampson with a few eccentricities of his own. These include a misogyny that is not entirely gratuitous, for he once suffered disappointment in love.

Oldbuck is a success—entertainingly garrulous when he finds an audience, and at times capable of a noble but cantankerous pessimism. Of interest is the way in which he reveals man's traditional contentiousness in a new form. As a peaceable student of the past he may " detest a drum like a Quaker," [21] but antiquaries, like modern litigants, fight old battles in modern dress. Thus Oldbuck and Wardour, who pretends to be a scholar himself, conduct an argument over the origins of a word like a trial at arms, choosing Lovel as judge :

> " Truly, gentlemen," said Lovel, " before you muster your forces and overwhelm me with authorities I should like to know the word in dispute."
> " *Benval*," said both the disputants at once.
> " Which signifies *caput valli*," said Sir Arthur.

[21] *A.*, ch. 6.

" The head of the wall," echoed Oldbuck.

There was a deep pause. " It is rather a narrow foundation to build a hypothesis upon," observed the arbiter.

" Not a whit, not a whit," said Oldbuck ; " men fight best in a narrow ring : an inch is as good as a mile for a home-thrust." [22]

Oldbuck's conversation also reveals an aggressive fondness for keeping issues alive so that a " home-thrust " can be delivered whatever the circumstances. In the episode in which Wardour, his daughter, and Ochiltree are rescued from the narrow sands before the rising and stormy tide, he cannot refrain from making fun of Wardour's Toryism and pride of ancestry :

"Right, right, that's right too ; I should like to see the son of Sir Gamelyn de Guardover on dry land myself. I have a notion he would sign the abjuration oath, and the Ragman Roll to boot, and acknowledge Queen Mary to be nothing better than she should be. . . . But he's safe now, and here a' comes—(for the chair was again lowered, and Sir Arthur made fast in it, without much conscious-ness on his own part)—here a' comes ; bowse away, my boys, canny wi' him. A pedigree of a hundred links is hanging on a tenpenny tow ; the whole barony of Knockwinnock depends on three plies of hemp ; *respice finem, respice funem*—look to your end, look to a rope's end. Welcome, welcome, my good old friend, to firm land. . . ." [23]

His disputatiousness is, of course, an ironic parody of the ancient forms of combat commemorated by his collection of old weapons. But there is a still deeper paradox in Oldbuck—one that sheds light on the nature of Scott's mind and on the peculiar character of the novel as a whole. Oldbuck is a Whig anti-quarian with ancestral roots in the German Reformation. He is thus committed to a certain generosity of opinion regarding

[22] *A.*, ch. 6.   [23] *A.*, ch. 8.

revolutionary movements. His view of the French Revolution is remarkably tolerant. It may be likened, he says, " to a storm or hurricane, which, passing over a region, does great damage in its passage, yet sweeps away stagnant and unwholesome vapours, and repays, in future health and fertility, its immediate desolation and ravage." [24]

These words are surprising in themselves. We may concede that they are Oldbuck's, not Scott's, that they are " in character," and that there is a touch of satire in Scott's presentation. Nevertheless, Oldbuck is a fundamentally humane and sympathetic person, very much an object of Scott's affection. And his speech which we would expect to excite opposition, receives no refutation. Whatever Scott may have said when he was " on the cry " against the Whigs and Radicals of his day, his fictional imagination was too generous and unpredictable to submit everlastingly to the ideological clichés of the Tory mind.

The essential point about Oldbuck's speech on the revolution, however, is that it reveals him as a personality at crosspurposes. On the one hand, he has an intense desire to preserve the past, to decipher inscriptions, to trace the Romans in Scotland, to revive the epic in the form of a grand *Caledoniad*; on the other, he ridicules ancestor-worship, accepts social changes that may lead to that defacement of monuments which, as an antiquarian, he is committed to deplore, and scorns Tory fears of change. His politics and his hobby-horse are at odds.

In this respect Oldbuck is well suited to be the central figure of *The Antiquary*, for this, more than any other, is Scott's novel of dissociation. The number of instances where " heterogeneous elements are yoked by violence together " is striking. Consider the following catalogue of discordant juxtapositions and " purposes mistook " :

1. While Oldbuck is explaining to Lovel why he believes that a certain ditch is the remnant of a praetorian fortification, Edie Ochiltree enters and remarks, " Praetorian here, praetorian there, I mind the bigging o't." He then reveals that the ditch is actually the remnant of a shelter that he and his companions

[24] *A.*, ch. 35.

built there only twenty years before. There is something
similar to Dominie Sampson's confrontation of Meg in this
scene, but there is also much more. Edie's revelation is both
comical and cruel. Since Oldbuck's theory has been presented in a very learned manner, the effect of the interruption is
to raise doubts about the whole apparatus of antiquarian
investigation. The sting can still be felt.[25]

2. The distance between the antiquarian and the objects of his
investigation is re-emphasised in the scene in which Elspeth
sings the ballad of " Red Harlaw." Oldbuck's learning is
rich and extensive; Elspeth's mind, in her grief and senility,
is as narrowly focused as a mind can be. But she knows
antiquity in a way that Oldbuck, scribbling his notes, will
never master.[26]

3. While on a picnic at which Dousterswivel is present, Lovel
reads Isabella Wardour's German tale of a Harz mountain
demon who leads a young man to riches and to death. The
tale is an example of genuine supernaturalism beside which
Dousterswivel's mumbo-jumbo seems cheap and ridiculous.
The theme of human greed seeking and receiving super-
natural aid parallels the efforts of Sir Arthur Wardour to find
treasure with Dousterswivel's magical assistance, but Sir
Arthur is too foolish a gull, and Dousterswivel too
transparent a quack, to be convincing. The distance in
tone and dignity between Isabella's story and the Wardour-
Dousterswivel plot is almost too wide for irony to function.[27]

4. Hector M'Intyre, Oldbuck's Highland nephew, is a well-
meaning young man who happens to have a hot temper.
He challenges Lovel to a duel on grounds that are almost
totally obscure. The result is an unnatural " private war "
between two men of goodwill in a peaceful landscape.
Lovel wounds M'Intyre and leaves the scene crushed by
feelings of guilt, not to return until the end of the novel.
Hector (the name is intended to be ironic) later engages in
another personal combat—this time with a seal! Again he is

[25] *A.*, ch. 4.   [26] *A.*, ch. 40.
[27] *A.*, ch. 18.

defeated, despite his being motivated (literally) by a spirit of
Ossianic derring-do. To such a sputtering end have come
the fiery traditions of the Highlands.[28]

5. The disappearance of Lovel, though not permanent, has a
strange near-parallel in the death of Steenie Mucklebackit, a
young fisherman whose relationship with Oldbuck's maid
promises to become an engaging lower-class echo of the
love-story of Lovel and Isabella Wardour. Steenie's death
at sea is sudden, unexpected, and gratuitous.[29]

6. When the Mucklebackit cottage is in deep mourning as preparations for the funeral of Steenie are underway, old Elspeth
raises her glass " and, as the smile of dotage played upon her
shrivelled features, she pronounced, with a hollow and
tremulous voice, ' Wishing a' your healths, sirs, and often
may we hae such merry meetings! ' " [30]

7. Not only is the solemn parade of the Glenallan story out of
keeping with the atmosphere of Oldbuck's environment, but
the tragedy is peculiar in that Glenallan's years of penance
were totally unnecessary. There was no incest.[31]

8. At the end of the novel all conflicts are resolved and the
hero, resplendent in a uniform that symbolises his assured
status, is restored to his inheritance and his beloved. The
occasion of his re-emergence is the news that a French invasion is imminent. But the report is untrue. *The Antiquary*
concludes with a splendid false alarm.[32]

9. This false alarm is just one symptom of the unreliability of
systems of transport and communication in *The Antiquary*.
The novel abounds in messages delayed or misunderstood,
in journeys interrupted or diverted. In the delightful first
chapter the coach from Edinburgh to Queensferry is delayed,
causing Lovel and Oldbuck to miss the tide. This pattern
continues. The walk of Isabella and her father along the
sands near Fairport is violently interrupted by a storm.[33]
Even the ubiquitous Edie has trouble. The coach that he
requires to carry him to Tannonburgh on his mission of

[28] *A.*, chs. 20, 30.   [29] *A.*, ch. 29.   [30] *A.*, ch. 31.
[31] *A.*, ch. 33.   [32] *A.*, ch. 45.   [33] *A.*, ch. 7.

D

rescue for the Wardour estate overturns.[34]   The personality
of Hector is unusually well suited to such a world, for he
moves in fits and starts.   His arrival at Fairport is sudden,
and he twice turns off his road in order to pick quarrels.[35]
As for channels of information—they are not to be trusted.
The all-important Glenallan story barely makes its way
across the blank areas in the memory of the senile Elspeth.[36]
The Fairport post office, the centre of this world of broken
threads, is under the command of Mrs Mailsetter.   Her
purpose is not to transmit letters, but to relish scandal, even
to the extent of conniving at the breaking of seals.   At one
time she sends a girl away disappointed, even though the
love-letter she awaits is before her in the post office.   When
an urgent express letter arrives for Lovel, she assigns the
delivery of it to her ten-year-old son, who hasn't the faintest
idea how to manage the pony he is to ride, and who must be
rescued from disaster by Edie.[37]   And even if the mail is
delivered, it need not be read.   Sir Arthur Wardour simply
refuses to open the letters of his creditors.[38]   It is surely
fitting that the abortive mobilisation at the end of the novel
is the result of the mishandling of a system of signals.

These anticlimaxes, dissonances, obscurities suggest a sort of
careless mannerism, as though Scott were mocking the whole
idea of cohesion and perspective.   Perhaps there is some explanation of these discords in the position of *The Antiquary* in relation
to its predecessors.   " *Waverley*," wrote Scott in his introduction,
" embraced the age of our fathers, *Guy Mannering* that of our
own youth, and the *Antiquary* refers to the last ten years of the
eighteenth century."   Of the three novels, the first is well
designed in the conventional sense, the second less so, the third
least of all.   It would seem that the closer Scott came to his own
age the more chaotic the world became for him.   Even in the
civil wars of the past there was an order that he could not see in
the world around him.   But we must add to this possibility a

[34] *A.*, ch. 41.   [35] *A.*, chs. 19 and 30.   [36] *A.*, ch. 33.
[37] *A.*, ch. 15.   [38] *A.*, ch. 41.

further paradox—that Oldbuck, the authority on the past, does not know the past. Scott as a historical thinker quite casually and humorously confronts us with a rather sophisticated dilemma : that the impulse to study the past may involve the use of tools that in themselves remove the past farther from us. Few contemporary historians have failed to be puzzled by this problem, and to know that they are being puzzled.

When its discords emerge in a comic context *The Antiquary* is at its best, as when Oldbuck, awakened by the news of an impending invasion, prepares for battle :

Our Antiquary, his head wrapped warm in two double night-caps, was quietly enjoying his repose, when it was suddenly broken by the screams of his sister, his niece, and two maid-servants.

" What the devil is the matter ? " said he, starting up in his bed ; " womankind in my room at this hour of night! are ye all mad ? "

" The beacon, uncle! " said Miss M'Intyre.

" The French coming to murder us! " screamed Miss Griselda.

" The beacon, the beacon! the French, the French! murder, murder! and waur than murder!" cried the two hand-maidens, like the chorus of an opera.

" The French ! " said Oldbuck, starting up. " Get out of the room, womankind that you are, till I get my things on. And, hark ye, bring me my sword."

" Whilk o' them, Monkbarns? " cried his sister, offering a Roman falchion of brass with the one hand, with the other an Andrea Ferrarra without a handle.

" The langest, the langest," cried Jenny Rintherout, dragging in a two-handed sword of the twelfth century.

" Womankind," said Oldbuck, in great agitation, " be composed, and do not give way to vain terror. Are you sure they are come ? " [39]

Jenny is " sure they are come," but she is wrong. The warning beacon was manned by old Caxon, Oldbuck's barber.

[39] *A.*, ch. 45.

Caxon's chief interest in life is the care of wigs, and decadent Fairport has only three left for him to nurture, one of them Oldbuck's.[40] The old man mistakes a bonfire made of the remains of the discredited Dousterswivel's mining apparatus for a warning signal, and as a result Scotland springs to arms.

The Antiquary is a very odd novel.

[40] *A.,* ch. 5.

4

THE BLACK DWARF
&
OLD MORTALITY

" As to Covenanters and Malignants they were both
a set of cruel and bloody bigots and had notwithstanding those virtues with which bigotry is
sometimes allied. . . . Neither had the least idea
either of toleration or humanity so that it happens
that so far as they can be distinguished from each
other one is tempted to hate most the party which
chances to be uppermost for the time."

— Scott, letter to John Richardson

" Eh, sirs ! yon's a awfu' sight, and yet ane canna
keep their een aff frae it ! "

— Cuddie Headrigg

In December 1816, only six months after the publication of
The Antiquary, the bookstalls were displaying two new Scott
novels, *The Black Dwarf* and *Old Mortality*. Seldom has an
author offered so unequal a pairing. The first is an abortive
attempt to build a story around a deformed misanthrope who
longs for affection and who commits several acts of unexpected
benevolence. Whatever virtues may be found in peripheral

scenes or characters, the Dwarf is central, and he is a failure. Here is an example of his speech :

> " Let Destiny drive forth her scythed car through the overwhelmed and trembling mass of humanity! Shall I be the idiot to throw this decrepit form, this misshapen lump of mortality, under her wheels, that the Dwarf, the Wizard, the Hunchback may save from destruction some fair form or some active frame, and all the world clap their hands at the exchange ? No, never ! " [1]

We may hope that Scott grew tired of such nonsense. He tells us in his introduction that a friend (probably the Edinburgh publisher Blackwood) persuaded him " that the idea of the Solitary was of a kind too revolting, and more likely to disgust than to interest the reader." The real truth is more characteristic of Scott : he first had an outburst of very bad temper over this criticism, but he soon gave in, devised a hasty conclusion, and allowed the novel to make its way on the market as well as it could.[2]

The Black Dwarf, however, is no exception to the rule that an author's failures can be as instructive as his successes. The Dwarf's language, of which the above example is typical, is Wardour Street Augustan, full of windy abstractions that have no referential force or exactitude. Part of the reason for this stylistic failure is the Dwarf's place in history. This place is, quite truthfully, nowhere. Misanthropy involves the cutting of all ties. For Scott, however, man was a social animal. The loyalties that give vitality to Fergus MacIvor or the Baron of Bradwardine, the commitments to socially existing styles of life that make Meg Merrilies and Edie Ochiltree meaningful to us, are life-giving properties. The Dwarf, in abandoning such connexions, abandons life itself and becomes a congregation of vapours.

The question remains why Scott should have attempted a misanthrope at all. I suspect there was more than wayward mis-

---

[1] *B.D.,* ch. 6.

[2] *Letters,* IV. 276 ; H. J. C. Grierson, *Sir Walter Scott, Bart : A New Life, Supplementary to, and Corrective of, Lockhart's Biography,* London 1938, pp. 136-9.

calculation behind his choice. For the Dwarf, in a perverse way, represents an effort at transcendence. His misanthropy has something in common with Joshua Geddes's quietism in *Redgauntlet*—it is above the battles of Whig and Tory, Hanoverian and Jacobite. As his *Journal* testifies, there was that in the world's first true political novelist which longed for the death of politics in the modern sense.[3] The low characters, content with their earthy and pragmatic good sense, are evidence of this longing. So are the saints and the recluses. Uninteresting in himself, the Dwarf has some interesting company.

Of one thing we may be certain : if the Dwarf were set down in the world of *Old Mortality*, he would lose what sanity he possesses. In this impressive and strenuous work doctrine and party are the forces that very nearly ride Scotland to her death. Like *Waverley* in breadth of scope and seriousness of presentation, it goes beyond *Waverley* in the degree to which it saturates the affairs of ordinary life with political significance. Like *Waverley* also, it succeeds because in it the depth of Scott's concern with one of the crises of British history is matched by the depth of his aesthetic commitment.

The structure of *Old Mortality* is as different as possible from the rambling plot of *The Antiquary*. Following E. M. W. Tillyard's advice that when reading Scott we must be ready for anything,[4] we discover that for nearly three-quarters of its length *Old Mortality* is the most Racinian novel in English. In the story of Henry Morton the classical conflict between love and loyalty—given sociological depth through Scott's understanding of the pressure of inherited ideological traditions—is realised in a plot that is clearly articulated, precisely balanced between its opposing forces, and sufficiently intense to convey the true agony of the divided impulses of the central figures.

The impression of structural firmness is enhanced by the massive clarity with which the novel builds itself around two major military events, the skirmish at Loudon Hill and the battle of Bothwell Bridge. In the first the Covenanters are the victors;

---

[3] *Journal*, 1. 74.
[4] E. M. W. Tillyard, *The Epic Strain in the English Novel*, p. 70.

in the second they are defeated. The whole plot progresses along lines suggested by this reversal. After the first engagement, the sense of cadence is especially firm, for Scott delivers judgment in a paragraph that is judicious, generous, and, above all, authoritative:

> And whatever may be thought of the extravagance or narrow-minded bigotry of many of their tenets, it is impossible to deny the praise of devoted courage to a few hundred peasants, who, without leaders, without money, without magazines, without any fixed plan of action, and almost without arms, borne out only by their innate zeal and a detestation of the oppression of their rulers, ventured to declare open war against an established government, supported by a regular army and the whole force of three kingdoms.[5]

There is, moreover, a dramatic economy in the earlier chapters that suggests that Scott, setting his jaw and getting on with his business, was determined to atone for the leisurely opening of *Waverley* once and for all. Thus he offers us a series of sharp, small-scale conflicts that imply in the clearest way the imminence of civil war. First there is the " wappenschaw," a shooting match that is at once a gesture of obedience to the King at a time of unrest and an excellent opportunity for Henry Morton to make a striking entrance.[6] Shortly thereafter Morton encounters Balfour of Burley, the fanatical leader of the Covenanters, fresh from the murder of an Archbishop, and watches him wrestle with the Cavalier trooper Bothwell in a match that foreshadows the later deadly combat at Loudon Hill.[7] Soon follow the incident at Milnwood in which Morton gives sanctuary to Burley,[8] the scene of Mause Headrigg's dismissal at Tillietudlem,[9] the arrest of Morton at Milnwood,[10] and the introduction of the awesome Claverhouse.[11] The style of these early chapters abandons leisure for efficiency:

[5] *O.M.*, ch. 18. [6] *O.M.*, ch. 3. [7] *O.M.*, ch. 4.
[8] *O.M.*, ch. 5. [9] *O.M.*, ch. 7. [10] *O.M.*, ch. 8.
[11] *O.M.*, ch. 11.

He pointed towards a pass leading up into a wild
extent of dreary and desolate hills; but as he was about
to turn his horse's head into the rugged path which led
from the highroad in that direction, an old woman wrapped
in a red cloak, who was sitting by the cross-way, arose,
and approaching him, said, in a mysterious tone of voice,
" If ye be of our ain folk, gangna up the pass the night
for your lives. There is a lion in the path that is there.
The curate of Brotherstane and ten soldiers hae beset the
pass to hae the lives of ony of our puir wanderers that
venture that gate to join wi' Hamilton and Dingwall." [12]

This passage has its rewarding details—the very tortuousness
of the first sentence accords with the darkness of the path and the
mystery of the woman's presence; the redness of her cloak
symbolises the threat of bloodshed; the ironic name of the
curate's parish and the cryptic use of the Scriptural quotation
intensify our awareness of danger and insane fanaticism.

The dramatic sharpness of such scenes is well suited to a novel
in which political and religious divisions are stark and absolute.
For the principals society provides no genial middle ground,
and Scott sadly reinforces their dilemma by invoking *l'esprit de
géométrie* and balancing his groups of characters in a way that
might make the reader suspect that there is almost too much
pattern. He seems determined to give a detailed embodiment of
the attitude he expressed in the letter to John Richardson quoted
at the beginning of this chapter. Covenanters and Malignants
are thus arranged in order of ferocity. Among the former are
moderates like Poundtext, compulsive doctrinaires like Kettledrummle and the comical Mause Headrigg, poetical zealots like
Ephraim Macbriar, and madmen like Habakkuk Mucklewrath.
(In his own criticism of *Old Mortality* in the *Quarterly Review*
Scott refers to the graded enthusiasms of the Presbyterians in a
manner that clearly indicates a considerable degree of conscious
intent.) [13] There are similar stages of fanaticism among the
Royalists. In ascending order, we have Lord Evandale, Major

<hr/>

[12] *O.M.*, ch. 5.   [13] *Quarterly Review*, XVI (1817), p. 461.

Bellenden, Lady Bellenden, Sergeant Bothwell, Claverhouse, and the extremely cruel Dalzell. Fortunately for the novel, characters do not reflect each other too exactly across the political gulf, but even so there are some reasonably close correspondences. Morton and Evandale are both honourable and decent moderates on opposite sides. Burley and Claverhouse form so obvious a polarity that we are not surprised to find them eventually joining forces for expediency's sake.[14] Lady Bellenden and Mause Headrigg, despite their difference in rank, are examples of doctrinaire automatism; just as the one can easily be triggered into spouting Scripture,[15] so the other can be set off on the subject of King Charles' breakfast at Tillietudlem with such ease that the tag eventually becomes a bore.[16] Furthermore the soldiers of each side resemble each other in their tendency to become mutinous when not controlled with a firm hand. Before Bothwell Bridge the Covenanters become hopelessly divided between moderates and extremists when Morton is absent,[17] just as the dragoons mutiny when Evandale is away. [18]

There is similar artifice in the love-stories of *Old Mortality*. As generous rivals for the hand of Edith, Henry Morton and Lord Evandale convey reciprocal benefits as though they were engaged in an honourable *pas de deux*. First Evandale saves Morton from execution,[19] then Morton rescues Evandale after Drumclog,[20] and again releases him from Burley's threats to slay him as a hostage.[21] Finally, the novel concludes as the dying Evandale joins Morton's and Edith's hands.

There is, moreover, a sustained similarity, already noticed by Alexander Welsh,[22] between the love-stories of Henry and Edith and Cuddie and Jenny Dennison. Here the device of parallel plotting is employed with considerable exactness. All four of these characters form a square of their own between the massive

[14] *O.M.*, ch. 42.   [15] *O.M.*, ch. 8.   [16] *O.M.*, ch. 3.
[17] *O.M.*, ch. 31.   [18] *O.M.*, ch. 28.   [19] *O.M.*, ch. 13.
[20] *O.M.*, ch. 17.   [21] *O.M.*, ch. 27.
[22] A. Welsh, *The Hero of the Waverley Novels*, New Haven and London, 1963, p. 233.

forces of dedicated men on either side. But just as Henry's love
for Edith is thwarted by his adherence to inherited principles,
so Cuddie's affection for Jenny must triumph over the hindrances
imposed by his mother's zeal for the Covenant and his role as
Henry's servant. There is even a similarity in the two women's
use of third parties to further their lovers' fortunes. Jenny
manipulates the devoted Tam Halliday for Cuddie's sake; Edith,
with considerable moral reservations, uses Evandale to save
Morton. Both Morton and Cuddie become jealous as a consequence. Scott clearly invites us to consider the two situations
side by side, for after Cuddie has told Morton of Jenny's employment of Halliday for his sake, we read the following :

> There was here a deep and long pause. Cuddie was
> probably engaged in regretting the rejection of his
> mistress's bounty, and Henry Morton in considering from
> what motives, or upon what conditions, Miss Bellenden
> had succeeded in procuring the interference of Lord
> Evandale in his favour.[23]

There is, however, a significant difference between the two
pairs of lovers—a difference sharp enough to convey a sense of
balance through contrast. Between Henry and Edith lies the
perilous question of political principle. Cuddie, on the other
hand, is a cautious pragmatist, aware at the battle of Loudon Hill
that even Presbyterian bullets may forget the Covenant and
accidentally strike down his sermonising mother,[24] while Jenny,
who would fit well into Shaw's *Man and Superman* as an embodiment of the sort of feminine purposefulness that reduces
" ideas " to irrelevance, knows that " it's maybe as weel to hae a
friend on baith sides." [25] The rather breathy and stammering
argument between Henry and Edith that takes place as he con-
ducts her party to safety from their castle [26] is, to their great
advantage, beyond the range of the two servants. Hence the
suitability and importance of Mause. As the most thoroughly
saturated doctrinaire that Scott ever found among the common

[23] *O.M.*, ch. 14.   [24] *O.M.*, ch. 17.   [25] *O.M.*, ch. 24.
[26] *O.M.*, ch. 29.

people, she is the link between the fortunes of the two pairs of lovers, for it is through her volcanic zeal that Cuddie is separated from the Bellendens and joined in fate with Morton.[27]

The difference in the degree of political passion between the two pairs of lovers is emphasized by Scott's abandonment of the device of the two heroines. Unlike Edward Waverley, Morton is a mature hero who has no erotic choice; for him it is Edith or no-one. Scott is thus encouraged to develop the possibility of political disagreement as a major impediment to the union of lovers. In so doing he takes an original and significant step. British novelists before Scott had found the most formidable obstacles to the fulfilment of love in the class structure. The question of status is crucial in works as divergent as *Pamela*, *Joseph Andrews*, *Cecilia*, and *Pride and Prejudice*. But the old contest between snobs and climbers, so rich in possibilities for other writers, did not stimulate Scott's imagination. We need only compare Mrs Bennett with Gilbert Glossin to see this, remembering that Glossin is a comparatively rare type in the Waverley Novels. Scott preferred to maintain firm distinctions in " rank " and then, as Waverley's servant Alick Polworth demonstrates, allow one rank to judge the other. Social impediments to love in Scott are primarily horizontal, not vertical; they involve national, religious or political differences.

The example of Chateaubriand is in itself enough to remind us that Scott was not entirely original in this shift of direction, and there had been anticipations closer to home. Charlotte Smith, in *The Young Philosopher*, had married her English heroine to an impoverished Highlander with some uncomfortable consequences, and later Maria Edgeworth combined feelings of class and national inferiority in Lady Clonbrony of *The Absentee*.[28] Earlier still the American Revolution had inflicted an anguished separation upon the two lovers of S. J. Pratt's subliterary *Emma Corbett*.[29] Where Scott differs from such writers is in the relent-

---

[27] *O.M.*, ch. 8.

[28] *The Young Philosopher* (London 1798); *Tales of Fashionable Life*, 6 vols., London 1809–12, Vol. VI.

[29] S. J. Pratt, *Emma Corbett : or the Miseries of Civil War*, Dublin 1780.

lessness with which a difference of political affiliation invades the
nervous system and joins other psycho-erotic forces as an equal
contestant in the emotional conflicts of a love-story. Thus when
Edith, after a desperate resistance, has to accept Jenny Dennison's
information that Morton has indeed joined the rebels, her reaction
is hysterical:

> Her complexion became as pale as a corpse, her respiration
> so difficult that it was on the point of altogether failing
> her, and her limbs so incapable of supporting her that she
> sunk, rather than sat, down upon one of the seats in the
> hall, and seemed on the eve of fainting.[30]

Edith's response here is commensurate with that of Sophia
Western betrayed, or more appropriately still, of Pamela in
distress. No wonder that V. S. Pritchett saw in Scott a counterpart of Richardson in the political sphere.[31] Flawlessly chaste,
as befits a Scott hero, Henry Morton is none the less, in the eyes
of Edith, an ideological profligate—a political adulterer.

This emphasis on the emotional importance of political
opinion actually contributes to the novel's impression of structural balance, for it can produce within the mind of a character
a division between equiponderant forces that echoes the situation
within the realm. Edith may condemn Henry's actions and
resolve to " cast him off for ever," [32] but her future course will
waver between attraction and repulsion, just as the fortunes of
war waver between Covenanters and Royalists.

We may object that Scott, in applying so relentlessly the
structural and psychological principles of balance, antithesis, and
parallelism, was invoking the spirit of geometry to no good effect.
But the truth is that the vigour of *Old Mortality* is not in the least
impaired by these indications of blueprinting. Not only is the
working narrative style as direct as any that Scott was to produce,
but the speech of the characters possesses a vitality he was never

---

[30] *O.M.*, ch. 24.
[31] V. S. Pritchett, *The Living Novel*, London 1946, p. 57.
[32] *O.M.* ch. 42.

to excel. Here is Mause rejoicing over the rebels' victory at Loudon Hill, with her son's reply :

"They flee ! they flee ! . . . O, the truculent tyrants ! they are riding now as they never rode before. O, the false Egyptians, the proud Assyrians, the Philistines, the Moabites, the Edomites, the Ishmaelites ! The Lord has brought sharp swords upon them to make them food for the fowls of heaven and the beasts of the field. See how the clouds roll and the fire flashes ahint them, and goes forth before the chosen of the Covenant, e'en like the pillar o' cloud and the pillar o' flame that led the people of Israel out o' the land of Egypt ! This is indeed a day of deliverance to the righteous, a day of pouring out of wrath to the persecutors and the ungodly ! "

"Lord save us, mither," said Cuddie, " haud the clavering tongue o' ye, and lie down ahint the cairn, like Kettledrummle, honest man ! The Whigamore bullets ken unco little discretion, and will just as sune knock out the harns o' a psalm-singing auld wife as a swearing dragoon." [33]

We are accustomed to satisfaction from Scott's use of the Scottish vernacular, but he also worked remarkably well with the speech of the Restoration rakehells who followed Claverhouse. Scott had some of Joyce's ability to catch the tune of English writing in different periods. (He reaches his limit in the Elizabethan era; that is why the fools and swineherds of *Ivanhoe* speak Elizabethan English garnished with a few medievalisms.) [34] The experience of editing such works of Dryden as *The Spanish Friar* had acquainted Scott with the characteristic Cavalier rhetoric of mock-surprise at the inconsistencies of professed saints. When Mause, who has been represented to Bothwell as stone deaf, suddenly bursts out in denunciation of the government's test-oath, Bothwell's answer shows contempt for Roundhead deviousness in authentic terms :

[33] *O.M.*, ch. 17.
[34] See E. M. W. Tillyard, " Scott's Linguistic Vagaries," in *Essays Literary and Educational*, London 1962, pp. 99-107.

" Eh ! what, good dame ? . . . Here's a Whig miracle,
egad ! the old wife has got both her ears and tongue, and
we are like to be driven deaf in our turn. . . ." [35]

With epic speeches of a more extended and resonant nature,
where the reader may well be alert for bombast, Scott is at his best
among the Covenanters, with their habitual and effective use of
Scriptural speech patterns. Here are two examples—one by
Ephraim Macbriar after the victory at Loudon Hill, the other by
Burley as he answers an envoy's summons to surrender :

" Heaven has been with you and has broken the bow
of the mighty; then let every man's heart be as the heart
of the valiant Maccabeus, every man's hand as the hand of
the mighty Sampson, every man's sword as that of Gideon,
which turned not back from the slaughter ; for the banner
of reformation is spread abroad on the mountains in its
first loveliness, and the gates of hell shall not prevail
against it." [36]

" In one word, then . . . we are here with our swords on
our thighs, as men that watch in the night. We will take
one part and portion together as brethren in righteousness.
Whosoever assails us in our good cause, his blood be on
his own head. So return to them that sent thee, and God
give them and thee a sight of the evil of your ways ! " [37]

There is a point, however, where the fusion of verbal energy
and structural clarity that distinguishes *Old Mortality* breaks
down. It occurs after Ch. 36, in which we witness the trial of the
rebels by the Privy Council in Edinburgh. Morton is exiled, and
the next chapter brings him back after a ten years' absence.
Alexander Welsh, whose analysis of *Old Mortality* is exception-
ally adroit and attentive, summarises the symptoms of narrative
disintegration as follows :

The gratuitous promotion of the hero, his return as a
wandering stranger, the unbelievable " ghost " scene, the

[35] *O.M.*, ch. 8.   [36] *O.M.*, ch. 18.   [37] *O.M.*, ch. 16.

unspoken parallels to Odysseus but also to Hamlet, the
sudden introduction of a new villain, the patience of
Evandale, the fidelity of Edith, and the obliteration of
Burley in a mist of Satanism and sublime nature. . . .[38]

Welsh also observes that Basil Olifant, the " new villain," is
not presented to the reader's view until he is killed at the end of
the novel. And yet another peculiar circumstance may be added
to his list—the strange political behaviour of Evandale. Patient
as he is in enduring Edith's reluctance to marry (she becomes
impossibly frosty and negative in her responses), he is curiously
impulsive in his insistence on joining the Royalist rebels who are
dissatisfied with the consequences of 1688. Despite his sense of
loyalty to the Stuarts and to Claverhouse, his distinguishing
mark has been his moderation as a counterpart of Morton on the
Government side.[39] Now he plans to fight against the new
government, whose liberal and constitutional policies he must
surely have welcomed.[40] It is a sad inconsistency, and we
wonder whether Scott is writing under a desperate desire to get
Evandale out of the way by fair means or foul.

Clearly Scott is in trouble in these last chapters, and the
trouble is deep enough to encourage an examination of whatever
assumptions he may have held that could be responsible for his
confusion. According to Welsh, the root of the difficulty is
Morton himself. Trapped in a dilemma that he shares with most
of Scott's heroes, he is called upon to act—to be a true hero—
at the same time that he is required to embody a Burkian ideal of
passive, property-centred acquiescence in the decrees of law and
fate. Thus he must win Edith by accident or not at all. Prescrip-
tion is the rule; acquisitiveness, whether erotic or economic, is
ungentlemanly.[41]

Welsh's theory is well-argued. Certainly Morton's willing-
ness to give up Edith to Evandale even after realising that it is he

[38] A. Welsh, *The Hero of the Waverley Novels*, p. 256.
[39] *O.M.*, ch. 25.
[40] *O.M.*, ch. 38.
[41] See A. Welsh, *The Hero of the Waverley Novels*, esp. chs. 4 and 9.

she still loves carries self-denial to extreme lengths.[42] Yet I have difficulty accepting Welsh's explanation. It fails too drastically to account for the totality of my response to Morton's situation, character, and historical role. Not only, as Welsh acknowledges, is he one of Scott's more active heroes,[43] but there is a dedication even in Scott's presentation of him as a lover that at times triumphs over the etiquette-book style he usually employs for such matters. Morton's response to Edith's visit when he is imprisoned and awaiting a possible sentence of execution is an example :

> " How or why [asks Edith] is this imprisonment ? Can my uncle, who thinks so highly of you—can your own kinsman, Milnwood, be of no use ? are there no means ? and what is likely to be the event ? "
>
> " Be what it will," answered Henry, contriving to make himself master of the hand that had escaped from him, but which was now again abandoned to his clasp—" be what it will, it is to me from this moment the most welcome incident of a weary life. . . ." [44]

Scott's heroes talk to their women in a severely polite and formal style, but this should not obscure the vast difference between what is said here and what Lovel, for example, mutters to Miss Wardour in *The Antiquary*.

Again, I am moved by Morton's loneliness. Not only is he isolated by virtue of his humane view of political conflicts, he is also a particularly unhappy victim of Scott's customary father dilemma. Scott both disguises and intensifies this problem by having Henry's real father, an intelligent and courageous Presbyterian leader, die before the action begins, leaving Henry's uncle as guardian. Beside old Milnwood even Sir Richard Waverley seems graceful and enlightened. Scott describes him in a paragraph that is startling in its hostility and contempt :

The old gentleman had been remarkably tall in his earlier

[42] *O.M.*, ch. 39.
[43] A. Welsh, *The Hero of the Waverley Novels*, pp. 231-2.
[44] *O.M.*, ch. 10.

E

days, an advantage which he now lost by stooping to such
a degree that at a meeting, where there was some dispute
concerning the sort of arch which should be thrown over
a considerable brook, a facetious neighbour proposed to
offer Milnwood a handsome sum for his curved backbone,
alleging that he would sell anything that belonged to him.
Splay feet of unusual size, long thin hands garnished with
nails which seldom felt the steel, a wrinkled and puckered
visage, the length of which corresponded with that of his
person, together with a pair of little sharp bargain-making
grey eyes that seemed eternally looking out for their
advantage, completed the highly unpromising exterior of
Mr Morton of Milnwood. As it would have been very
injudicious to have lodged a liberal or benevolent disposition in such an unworthy cabinet, nature had suited his
person with a mind exactly in conformity with it—that is
to say, mean, selfish, and covetous.[45]

Separated from his father by such an image as this, surrounded by extremists of the worst sort, divided from Edith
Bellenden by physical and political barriers, Morton often resembles Edgar Ravenswood in *The Bride of Lammermoor*—a
victim of hard luck and historical conflict doomed to alienation
and exile in all their forms.

However, despite these disadvantages, once Morton joins the
Covenanters he becomes the only one of their leaders with the
steadiness required to confront the military difficulties that beset
them. Bedevilled by their factions, jealousies, and suspicions, he
not only devises a respectable strategy at Bothwell Bridge, but
rises to genuine and effective passion in his exhortation to combat:

" Hear me," he exclaimed, springing to the pulpit which
Mucklewrath had been compelled to evacuate by actual
exhaustion—" I bring from the enemy an offer to treat, if
you incline to lay down your arms. I can assure you the
means of making an honourable defence, if you are of more

[45] *O.M.*, ch. 6.

manly tempers. The time flies fast on. Let us resolve
either for peace or war ; and let it not be said of us in
future days, that six thousand Scottish men in arms had
neither courage to stand their ground and fight it out,
nor prudence to treat for peace, nor even the coward's
wisdom to retreat in good time and with safety. What
signifies quarrelling on minute points of church discipline,
when the whole edifice is threatened with total destruction ?
O, remember, my brethren, that the last and worst evil
which God brought upon the people whom He had once
chosen—the last and worst punishment of their blindness
and hardness of heart, was the bloody dissensions which
rent asunder their city, even when the enemy were
thundering at its gates ! " [46]

These words, as Welsh acknowledges,[47] inspire Burley himself
to action. When we consider the tendency of the Covenanters to
disintegrate into " hollow factions," and, on the other hand, the
readiness of the dragoons opposing them to mutiny unless firmly
governed, Morton's military persistence seems impressive by
contrast. Burdened by the inevitable intellectual difficulties of
the moderate man among fanatics, he none the less constitutes a
vital centre.

The problem of Scott's concluding chapters, however, remains. The difficulties here are not entirely without precedent.
For example, there are some interesting similarities between
Morton's situation and that of Edward Waverley. Each hero is
separated from the rebel forces with which he has been fighting,
finds powerful intercessors (Talbot and Claverhouse), witnesses
the trial of rebel leaders, and is finally manoeuvred into a wedding.
And in both novels there is a certain nervousness in the handling
of the narrative. Edward is moved rather relentlessly from place
to place ; Morton also travels widely, and, in addition, seems
strangely cursed with an inability to sit still. His old house-
keeper, Ailie Wilson, is understandably puzzled by his insistence

[46] O.M., ch. 31.
[47] A. Welsh, The Hero of the Waverley Novels, p. 232.

on leaving Milnwood almost as soon as he returns from the Continent in order to spend the night at Neil Blane's inn.[48] There seems no reason for his behaviour but sheer restlessness.

This restlessness, in addition to the oddities noted above, suggests that whatever difficulties Scott might have had in bringing *Waverley* to a harmonious conclusion became critical in *Old Mortality*.

I would like to propose three principal reasons for these difficulties : first, the peculiar historical significance of marriage in the Waverley Novels ; second, the problem of historical determinism and human ethical responsibility ; and third, the problem of historical reconciliation and synthesis. If all this seems too aggressively metaphysical to apply to a popular novelist who is merely trying to get his hero and heroine before the altar in a reasonably convincing manner, I can only reply that the persistence with which Scott sets the human will in conflict with the facts of historical turmoil and change is precisely the most striking thing about the Waverley Novels. It is an act of intellectual justice to accept Scott's historical preoccupations and to think about them as clearly as possible.

First, concerning marriage, Scott shared Jane Austen's implied view of the wedding as a ritual symbolising a difficult adjustment between a person and the social order. What Dorothy Van Ghent says of Elizabeth Bennett's world in *Pride and Prejudice* applies also to the world of Henry and Edith : ". . . marriage means a complex engagement between the marrying couple and society. . . . In marrying, the individual marries society as well as his mate." [49]

But the problem for the Scott hero and heroine becomes more complex still, for their marriage must represent an individual's successful adjustment to the powerful and apparently lawless currents of history (never more than a distant echo offstage in Jane Austen), and, because of the interdependence of political and erotic passion, it must symbolise a reconciliation between the

---

[48] *O.M.*, ch. 40.

[49] D. Van Ghent, *The English Novel : Form and Function*, New York, 1953, p. 102.

opposing political currents that make the pageants of history so bloody. If the Civil Wars had continued, Henry and Edith would never have wed at all. Here we see the importance of Scott's abandonment of the two heroines in *Old Mortality*. By taking this step, thus intensifying Morton's dilemma, he confronts him with a situation that Jane Austen's characters are not required to face. In one respect, at least, they are closer to Jenny Dennison, whose happy and sensible union with Cuddie contrasts so sharply with the situation of the more historically involved couple. In Scott, ideology tends to separate lovers, not to join them, and if they succeed in marrying, their identification with political and social interests almost turns them into allegorical symbols of the reconciliation of large historical forces. Thus the decision as to the " right time " for a wedding may be taken out of the hands of the hero and his heroine and determined by forces indifferent to their individual passions. In Ch. 12, Morton, whose jealousy of Evandale is exacerbated by his helpless situation as Claverhouse's prisoner, blames the " accursed tyranny " of the Government for the fact that he cannot plead for Edith's hand boldly and openly ; he then proceeds to blame himself for " being dead to public wrongs " in the past. His course is now clear. Rather than struggle with the immediate impediments to his union with Edith, he determines to join the Covenanters and bend history to his purposes. It is, to understate the matter, a rather arduous assignment, and *Old Mortality* actually represents the failure of Morton's efforts, culminating in a ten-year absence from Edith's neighbourhood. To bring Morton back after such a time and manage a wedding would tax the resources of any novelist. To be sure, after 1688 history may be said to have endorsed the union of Morton and Edith, but *Old Mortality* is, after all, a novel, not an allegory, and from the time Henry joins the Covenanters nearly every step he takes to make Scotland a safe place for men and women of good will adds to the distance to be made up between him and his beloved.

The second reason for Scott's difficulties in his concluding chapters lies in a characteristically ambivalent movement of

Scott's mind. The more he asserts the power of historical processes over areas of life not traditionally considered vulnerable
to them, the more he longs for transcendence. He is always on
the lookout for some particular attitude, belief, or social situation
that will possess a validity absolutely impervious to historical
change. His quest is in many ways a religious one, and an
important element of irony in *Old Mortality* derives from the
fact that only one of its many religious zealots, Bessie Maclure,
enters the realm of feeling where Christian ethics can operate
without the corruptions of sectarian rancour. Her brief account
to Morton of her reception of the wounded Evandale after
Bothwell Bridge is unique in the novel :

> " It's a lang story, sir. . . . But ae night, sax weeks or
> thereby afore Bothwell Brig, a young gentleman stopped
> at this puir cottage, stiff and bloody with wounds, pale
> and dune out wi' riding, and his horse sae weary he
> couldna drag ae foot after the other, and his foes were
> close ahint him, and he was ane o' our enemies. What
> could I do, sir ? You that's a sodger will think me but a
> silly auld wife ; but I fed him, and relieved him, and keepit
> him hidden till the pursuit was ower."
> " And who," said Morton, " dares disapprove of your
> having done so ? "
> " I kenna," answered the blind woman ; " I gat ill-will
> about it amang some o' our ain folk. They said I should
> hae been to him what Jael was to Sisera. But weel I wot
> I had nae divine command to shed blood, and to save it
> was baith like a woman and a Christian." [50]

For Henry and Edith, however, the transcendent principle is
the secular one of honour. Each is bound to Evandale by a
history of reciprocal obligation that neither can forget because
honour forbids. Hence that peculiar soliloquy of Morton's that
Welsh understandably finds so disturbing. Having overheard
Edith virtually confess to Evandale that she is still in love with

[50] *O.M.*, ch. 42.

him, Morton nevertheless represses his impulse to reveal himself
and claim her hand :

> " No, Edith ! " was his internal oath, " never will I add
> a thorn to thy pillow. That which Heaven has ordained,
> let it be ; and let me not add, by my selfish sorrows, one
> atom's weight to the burden thou hast to bear." [51]

I agree with Welsh that honour does indeed seem to resist
life and love together in this passage.[52] But I suspect that it is
really the apparent inexorability of historical processes that is
being resisted, and that the resistance is Scott's. By having
Morton refuse participation in the delights of marriage in a
settled kingdom in the name of a personal sense of obligation,
by binding Morton unmercifully to a code of self-sacrifice, Scott
is paradoxically defending human ethical freedom even in the
teeth of history's blessings. And because of this contradiction a
considerable amount of manipulation is required to bring the
lovers together, for what Morton denies to himself must be
granted him by circumstances.

The third reason for Scott's difficulties in bringing his novel
to a successful conclusion is related to the second. It lies in his
inability to envision a satisfactory historical synthesis after the
strenuous antitheses of the Civil War. It is obvious that man's
relationship to the processes of history is more problematical in
Old Mortality than in *Waverley*. The conclusion of the first
novel, with its atmosphere of reconciliation and compromise, is
more satisfying emotionally and aesthetically than that of *Old
Mortality*. Yet the Revolution of 1688 was reputed to be a
triumph of British political genius—a true victory of moderate
progressivism. Moreover, *Old Mortality* would appear to endorse the 1688 Revolution without qualification. Among the
opposing groups of characters it is the ideological " high-fliers "
who are the most inhumane. Absolutism and bloodlust go hand in
hand. Speaking as the omniscient author, Scott refers at the beginning of Ch. 37 to the " new era " inaugurated by the Revolution,

[51] *O.M.*, ch. 39.
[52] A. Welsh, *The Hero of the Waverley Novels*, p. 260.

to the "prudent tolerance of King William" which saved Scotland from "the horrors of a protracted civil war," to the revival of agriculture and the return of men to their normal pursuits. Where else would Scott find a better opportunity and incentive to overcome the impediments of time and distance and lead his lovers by easy stages to a condition of peaceful married happiness?

Karl Kroeber, in his study of the romantic writers as narrative artists, offers an explanation of Scott's fondness for straightforward narrative methods that, while increasing our sense of the awkwardness of *Old Mortality*'s conclusion, points the way to a clarification. Answering E. M. Forster's dismissal of Scott as a mere teller of tales,[53] Kroeber writes:

> The process of history works steadily in one direction only, and a more complex or dramatic representation of elements in the process than that provided by simple narrative would confuse the outline of the large development which it is Scott's purpose to portray.[54]

This explanation, with its emphasis on Scott's rejection of complexity, may seem to suit *The Lady of the Lake* better than *Old Mortality*, but we can, none the less, appreciate its relevance. The novel does indeed tell a story of a period that includes a major historical watershed, and the story moves with a clear and powerful logic and with considerable pleasure in its own narrative movement up to the time of Morton's exile. There is even a scene in the last chapter that seems to symbolise the movement of history away from an age of violence and intolerance. Burley and a dragoon, locked in a murderous wrestling match, are drowned in the Clyde. As the river flows indifferently on, the sense of history bringing such men to nought is inescapable. But if the Clyde flows smoothly, the story, as it approaches conclusion, does not.

Perhaps we may take a hint from Kroeber's linking of historical process with narrative movement and affirm that there was

[53] E. M. Forster, *Aspects of the Novel*, London 1927, pp. 46-56.
[54] K. Kroeber, *Romantic Narrative Art*, Madison (Wisconsin) 1960, p. 181.

something in Scott's imagination that stubbornly resisted the idea that 1688 marked a satisfying advance. The very splendour of the rhetoric of the militant Covenanters, when contrasted with the more modest discourse of moderate types such as Morton, Evandale, and Edith, seems to imply a characteristically " romantic " exaltation of energy over reason, of enthusiasm over prudence.

It may be possible to clarify Scott's implied doubts by refering to the Hegelian view of historical development. Scott has quite understandably been likened to Hegel. To raise historical processes to a level of great importance, to contrast characters who are significantly involved in these processes with those who are not, to portray a conflict between two opposing forces within a culture and to resolve that conflict by means of a settlement which, like the 1688 Revolution, was the basis of future institutions and values, is to make understandable Thomas Crawford's comment that " this most unmetaphysical of men actually did what Hegel, in Germany, was content merely to think." [55]

Yet Scott, when scrutinised, proves to be a rather slippery sort of Hegelian. Hegel's scheme of history is a pattern of progress, but the nearest Scott came to asserting that pattern was in *Waverley*, where the present triumphs over the past, finally adapting some of its values (loyalty, for example) to its own purposes and preserving others as aesthetic images. After *Waverley* Scott does not do what Hegel was content merely to think, for if thesis and antithesis are dramatically presented, the synthesis is blurred. It is significant that none of the major characters of *Old Mortality* seems willing to follow the counsel implied in Cuddie Headrigg's remark that " the country's weel eneuch, an it werena that dour deevil, Claver'se ... that's stirring about yet in the Highlands, they say, wi' a' the Donalds, and Duncans, and Dugalds that ever wore bottomless breeks driving about wi' him, to set things asteer again, now we hae gotten them a' reasonably weel settled." [56] We are not surprised at Claverhouse's legitimist fanaticism, nor at Burley's refusal to be tolerated, but these two are not alone. Evandale will not settle

[55] *Scott*, Edinburgh 1965, p. 48.   [56] *O.M.*, ch. 37.

down, Edith will not accept either of two highly attractive suitors, and Morton will not assert his rights as a preferred lover. In thus tormenting themselves, all three testify unmistakably to the irrelevance of the country's new-found peace for them. At this point—the year 1689—Scott's imagination balks at the prospect of a harmony between individual will and historical development, and, even at the cost of probability, disrupts the order of society, logic, and fiction.

He goes further; he rounds upon his own function and ridicules the conventions of the novel. In the brief " Conclusion " he shatters his mirror and leads us off to tea with an imaginary reader named Miss Buskbody. Her preferences, having been nurtured on such works as *Jemmy and Jenny Jessamy*, demand a happy ending. After Burley, Jenny Dennison, Macbriar and Claverhouse, we have this:

> " I love books which teach a proper deference in young
> persons to their parents. In a novel the young people
> may fall in love without their countenance, because it is
> essential to the necessary intricacy of the story, but they
> must always have the benefit of their consent at last. Even
> old Delville received Cecilia, though the daughter of a
> man of low birth." [57]

The irony here deepens with our awareness of what has gone before. Like the Ford car that stands outside the Bon Ton Store on Sinclair Lewis's *Main Street*, Miss Buskbody is the end result of centuries of human agony and endeavour. For a moment we see, as in a triple exposure, the discordant images of the epic heroes and saints, of Miss Buskbody, and of the author with his inner world of contradictory affections. Then, having been studiously polite to his hostess, he takes advantage of her momentary absence of mind and leaves. He is not yet of her world; there will be other excursions into the ages of poetry and violence.

[57] *O.M.*, " Conclusion."

5

ROB ROY

"Not know the figures of heraldry? of what
could your father be thinking?"
"Of the figures of arithmetic," I answered. . . .

— *Rob Roy*, Chapter 10

Like *Waverley* and *Old Mortality*, *Rob Roy* takes place against a
background of rebellion—in this instance the Jacobite uprising
of 1715—but it seems less serious than its two predecessors. For
one thing, it has a villain, Rashleigh Osbaldistone, whose per-
versities have no real historical cause. He is a literary villain,
temperamentally unprincipled and totally satanic. His stratagems
however, are of great importance to the plot, and for this reason
the events of the novel seem less dependent on historical convulsions than those of *Waverley* or *Old Mortality*. Furthermore,
the love-story of *Rob Roy*, though affected by political questions,
exists in a realm of its own. The heroine, Diana Vernon, is the
most dynamic of Scott's *ingénues*; the hero is intensely afflicted
with love-longing. The story of their love is tearful, " romantic,"
and poignantly entertaining.

There is, however, a serious and pervasive issue in *Rob Roy*,
an issue that gives the novel far more unity than it is sometimes
credited with.[1] *Rob Roy* is Scott's variation on the parable of the
Prodigal Son. Frank Osbaldistone, who tells his own story in

[1] See A. Welsh, *The Hero of the Waverley Novels*, p. 183.

retrospect, is a young Englishman with an appetite for freedom and adventure who quarrels with his father because he doesn't want to become a dull partner in the family's London trading firm. His refusal results in his being dispatched to his uncle's estate in Northumberland so that he may arrange for one of his cousins to fill the place first intended for him. While there he falls in love with Die Vernon and becomes rather indolent and irresponsible, until he suddenly discovers that his cousin and intended successor Rashleigh has stolen the bills upon which his father's concern depends for its commercial life. He then goes off to Glasgow and the Highlands. With the help of the Glasgow merchant Bailie Nicol Jarvie, the Highland outlaw Rob Roy, and Diana, he recovers the bills and is reconciled with his father. He finally falls heir to his uncle's estate and marries Die.

It is the issue of filial responsibility that unites *Rob Roy*. In his treatment of it Scott breaks new ground. Fathers and their surrogates in the previous novels were turned into objects of pity of condescension. In this way Scott's imagination exacted vengeance for the paternal rigours that had early in his life established a connexion between poetry and guilt. But such revenge was evasive, for Scott's father was no sneaking fellow like Sir Richard Waverley. He was honest, worthy, and narrowly respectable. In *Rob Roy* Scott confronts the father dilemma head-on, for if previous fathers had been too insignificant to quarrel with, William Osbaldistone is not. At the beginning of *Rob Roy* Frank resists his father strenuously and with full awareness of what he is doing—he is firmer here than anywhere else ! As a result he is, in effect, disinherited.

Rob Roy is no autobiography, but its first two chapters reflect a conflict of temperaments that can be discerned in accounts of Scott's early years. Frank writes verses ; his father has no liking for such things and expresses his distaste in a manner that would have suited the senior Scott : " To the memory of Edward the Black Prince. What's all this ? verses ! By Heaven, Frank, you are a greater blockhead than I supposed you ! " But Frank, like the young Scott, finds solace among women. He listens to the songs and stories of his old nurse with the same devotion that

Scott brought to his conversations with his imaginative mother.[2]
Frank also falls in love with a Jacobite, defends Catholics, and
develops a fondness for outlaws; in other words, he violates in
thought and deed precept after precept of the world of sane and
business-like Calvinism represented by his own father and the
author's. He even revolts against clear penmanship. Addressing
his son, William Osbaldistone complains :

> "—I wish, by the way, you would write a more distinct
> current hand, draw a score through the tops of your t's
> and open the loops of your l's. . . ." [3]

Anyone who has read any of Scott's manuscripts will recognise
and perhaps endorse this protest. Indeed he may already have
uttered it himself.

Frank's rebellion against his father opens a path for Rashleigh, whose manipulations bring the family's affairs to the edge
of ruin. When he learns of the possible effects of his stubborn-
ness, he expresses his remorse so intensely that he very nearly
accuses himself of parricide :

> " I grieve not for the loss, but for the effect which I know
> it will produce on the spirits and health of my father, to
> whom mercantile credit is as honour ; and who, if declared
> insolvent, would sink into the grave, oppressed by a sense
> of grief, remorse, and despair. . . . All this I might have
> prevented by a trifling sacrifice of the foolish pride and
> indolence which recoiled from sharing the labours of his
> honourable and useful profession." [4]

The novel would seem to endorse Frank's feeling of guilt, for
it gives emphasis to his rebellion by offering repeated examples
of filial obedience. Die Vernon not only gives her days and
nights to the protection of her father, she is also willing to
abandon the world for a convent in order to honour a commitment he has made.[5] Bailie Nicol Jarvie constantly refers to
" the deacon my father " as a source of the values he lives by.

---

2 *R.R.*, ch. 4 ; Lockhart, I. 20.   3 *R.R.*, ch. I.
    4 *R.R.*, ch. 17.   5 *R.R.*, ch. 37.

The sons of Rob Roy are similarly dedicated to the pursuit of
their father's way of life. Even when rebuked by their mother
for letting his enemies make off with him they accept the assumptions upon which her anger is based.[6] Rob himself, while com-
mendably interested in Frank's offer to help his sons make their
way in the world beyond the Highlands, preserves continuity
and rejects the offer.[7] One can hardly imagine his sons disobey-
ing him and carving out careers for themselves. Even the
cretinous offspring of Frank's north-country uncle make a
harmonious group with their father as they pursue the field sports
that he loves. One of the story's more nostalgic moments comes
with Frank's memory of the special attention that Sir Hildebrand
bestowed upon his favourite son Thorncliffe.[8] Only one of Sir
Hildebrand's sons deviates from the pattern, and that one is
Rashleigh, who is blamed for the deaths of his brothers and the
ruination of the estate.[9] We can better understand Frank's
frequent expressions of remorse when we consider that Sir
Hildebrand's death by spiritual and moral exhaustion can be
attributed to Rashleigh's betrayal of the family. Of the two
principal characters of the novel only Frank and his enemy
directly challenge the ideal of filial piety, and both raise the threat
of a father's death.

Frank, nevertheless, is no villain, but merely a proud and
rather callow young man who, despite his involvement in efforts
to recover his father's credit, actually assumes the role of a pilgrim
(or tourist) who observes various modes of existence until he is
at last ready to settle. Thus the question of filial loyalty is
closely bound up with the condition of the society in which he
lives. It is a fragmented world—one in which different ways of
life appeal to different appetites without answering the full needs
of the human personality. Scott actually brings Frank into
contact with five different styles of life before he allows him to
come to rest, and each system is found wanting.

Thus the world of business and commerce, which Scott treats
as a province or region like any other, at least in the early chapters,
is a Philistine world which exalts book-keeping over poetry,

[6] *R.R.*, ch. 31.   [7] *R.R.*, ch. 35.   [8] *R.R.*, ch. 37.   [9] *Ibid.*

action over contemplation. Moreover it is a community that has
a short way with nonconformists. Admirable as he may be in
many respects, William Osbaldistone's comments on his son's
poetic efforts are bigoted and cruel.

The second life-style is that of the country squire—the
province presided over by Sir Hildebrand and his sons. Sir
Hildebrand has his civilised moments, but the presiding deity of
Osbaldistone Hall is really Squire Western. Scott does well in
presenting the noisy brutishness of life among dogs, horses and
sportsmen :

> At length, while the dinner was, after various efforts,
> in the act of being arranged upon the board, " the clamour
> much of men and dogs," the cracking of whips, calculated
> for the intimidation of the latter, voices loud and high,
> steps which, impressed by the heavy-heeled boots of the
> period, clattered like those in the statue of the *Festin de
> pierre*, announced the arrival of those for whose benefit
> the preparations were made. The hubbub among the
> servants rather increased than diminished as this crisis
> approached : some called to make haste, others to take
> time, some exhorted to stand out of the way and make
> room for Sir Hildebrand and the young squires, some to
> close round the table and be *in* the way, some bawled to
> open, some to shut, a pair of folding-doors which divided
> the hall from a sort of gallery . . . or withdrawing-room,
> fitted up with black wainscot. Opened the doors were at
> length, and in rushed curs and men—eight dogs, the
> the domestic chaplain, the village doctor, my six cousins,
> and my uncle.[10]

With the unpleasant exception of Rashleigh the cousins
barely emerge as individuals from the welter of boorishness.
Die Vernon, who lives among them without sharing their values,
sums them up with sufficient contempt :

> " Percie, the son and heir, has more of the sot than of the
> gamekeeper, bully, horse-jockey, or fool. My precious

[10] *R.R.*, ch. 5.

Thornie is more of the bully than the sot, gamekeeper,
jockey, or fool. John, who sleeps whole weeks amongst
the hills, has most of the gamekeeper. The jockey is
powerful with Dickon, who rides two hundred miles
by day and night to be bought and sold at a horse-race.
And the fool predominates so much over Wilfred's other
qualities that he may be termed a fool positive." [11]

From this it is obvious that in leaving London Frank has ex-
changed one nest of Philistines for another. We are not surprised to learn that the most neglected room in Osbaldistone
Hall is the library,[12] hence its appropriateness as a rendezvous for
Frank and Diana. Both are romantic rebels against the stupidity
of their peers. For Frank the library becomes a warm and
intimate refuge from the clamour of businessmen and country
bloods where he and his lady can thumb the leaves of Ariosto
together.[13] Scott's early years taught him to associate poetry
with affectionate and indulgent women, and there is an element
of wish-fulfilment in Frank's experiences in the library. They
serve to emphasize that neither the commercial aristocracy nor
the squirearchy answer the emotional needs of imaginative young
men.

Frank observes other ways of life besides these. One of them
is Catholicism. This is not a subject that Scott usually handles
very well. Glenallan's spiritual agonies produce some of the least
effective moments in *The Antiquary*, for the reason that Scott is
inclined to become melodramatic in the Monk Lewis manner
whenever Catholics are introduced. Rashleigh, for example, is
the spidery Jesuit of literary tradition—soft-spoken, esoterically
learned, mysteriously influential, and sexually dangerous. Scott's
Journal, in which he calls Catholicism " a mean and depriving
superstition," shows that his portrayal of Rashleigh is in accord
with his prejudices.[14]

Nevertheless, Frank has defended Catholics to his father's
agent Owen,[15] and he eventually marries the Catholic Diana.

[11] *R.R.*, ch. 6.   [12] *R.R.*, ch. 10.   [13] *R.R.*, ch. 16.
[14] *Journal*, III. 27.   [15] *R.R.*, ch. 2.

And Die herself, badgered by intolerant Protestants like Jobson, becomes a sympathetic figure as she defends her persistence in her faith:

> "... it is hard that persons of birth and rank and estate should be subjected to the official impertinence of such a paltry pickthank as that, merely for believing as the whole world believed not much above a hundred years ago. ..." [16]

Here we see the cause of whatever sympathy for Catholicism managed to exist beside Scott's Protestant feelings. In the British area Catholicism was a party no longer in power—like Jacobitism, extreme Presbyterianism, or Scotland itself. This situation procured for the Catholics a certain minimal compassion, for one never-failing passport to Scott's sympathies was historical defeat. Hence Edward Glendinning's noble and pathetic speech in *The Abbot*, Ch. 14, a speech whose strongest appeal lies in its recollection of a past harmony between Church and people.

Despite conflicting impulses, however, Scott's final judgment of Catholicism is unfavourable. It is also perfectly consistent with his views of other religious groups, such as the Covenanters who murdered Archbishop Sharpe. Churches dedicated too strenuously to the transformation of the world inevitably become so worldly as they grapple with their enemies that they cease to serve as means of transcendence and become instead mere interested competitors in a historical struggle for power.

London commerce, Northumberland rusticity, Catholicism— these can be of little use to Frank. But there are two other areas remaining to be explored, both of them in Scotland. Frank's journey there introduces him to two sides of Scottish life—the Lowland area of Presbyterianism and trade represented by Bailie Nicol Jarvie, the Highland world of claymores and strong ancestral passions represented by Rob Roy and his family. It is here that Frank undergoes Edward Waverley's experience of seeing dreams become reality. Both of these young heroes are somewhat restless and quixotic. Despite his practical reasons

[16] *R.R.*, ch. 9.

for going into the Highlands on behalf of his father, Frank
reflects on what lies ahead in a way that indicates a degree of
romantic *ennui* sufficient to have turned him into a wanderer
whatever his circumstances :

> The peaks of this screen of mountains were as wildly
> varied and distinguished as the hills which we had seen
> on the right were tame and lumpish ; and while I gazed
> on this Alpine region I felt a longing to explore its recesses,
> though accompanied with toil and danger, similar to that
> which a sailor feels when he wishes for the risks and
> animation of a battle or a gale, in exchange for the
> insupportable monotony of a protracted calm.[17]

Frank's longing is soon answered. He witnesses at close
quarters the defeat of a party of redcoats by the MacGregors.
However, it is not the violence of the ambush that makes the
deepest impression on his mind, it is the death of Morris, the
terrified traitor whose information has led to the capture of Rob
Roy by his enemies. Here the novel reaches a climax. Morris's
execution is ordered by Rob Roy's wife Helen MacGregor. Like
Balfour and Claverhouse, she is one of Scott's polar figures—an
emblem of a way of life at its extremity. More desperate and
cruel than her husband, she orders Morris to be bound, weighted,
and thrown into a loch. The impression upon Frank is indelible :

> " He set up the most piercing and dreadful cries that fear
> ever uttered : I may well term them dreadful, for they
> haunted my sleep for years afterwards." [18]

This is emphatic language, but it is both appropriate and inevitable. Once again a romantic quest, begun in fantasy and the
fear of *ennui*, has led to an insupportable vision of violence.
Frank has overextended himself and must be pulled back. It is
not long before he is happily reunited with his father. What is
more, he learns at the time of the reunion that the crisis brought
on by Rashleigh's treachery would have yielded to his father's
mercantile skill and resolution without any touristic assistance

---

[17] *R.R.*, ch. 27.   [18] *R.R.*, ch. 31.

from his son. Frank does not seem noticeably chastened by this realisation, but the reader will take note of what is implied by Scott's account of the senior Osbaldistone's recent activities:

> When the tumult of joy was over I learnt that my father had arrived from Holland shortly after Owen had set off for Scotland. Determined and rapid in all his movements, he only stopped to provide the means of discharging the obligations incumbent on his house. By his extensive resources, with funds enlarged and credit fortified by eminent success in his continental speculation, he easily accomplished what perhaps his absence alone rendered difficult. . . .[19]

This passage very nearly reduces Frank to the level of an anti-hero. Forgotten is the hostility between father and son. The wheel is come full circle, and William Osbaldistone emerges as a hero of commerce. Business, after all, offers adventure enough for anyone in its speculative aspects. It is, in addition, a school of human nature, for " my father's perfect knowledge of mankind enabled him easily to appreciate the character of Andrew, and the real amount of his intelligence."[20] It is still more. The principle of honour, as important in *Rob Roy* as it is in *Old Mortality*, operates crucially in the mercantile world. As a possible response to the risks and near-disasters of speculative enterprise it sanctifies danger and acquisitiveness by associating them with the possibility of grace and self-denial. Thus William Osbaldistone is closer to the world of Rob Roy than would at first appear. The last we hear from Helen MacGregor is her expression of contempt for dishonour and her desire for vengeance. Osbaldistone knows both of these feelings, but he expresses them in more civilised ways. MacVittie and Company of Glasgow, in whom he had placed considerable trust, had disgracefully turned against him on the first sign of financial distress. When he is restored to solvency he writes them off and takes his business elsewhere. Here he operates according to the ideal of reciprocity that characterises the relationship between Waverley

[19] *R.R.*, ch. 36. [20] *Ibid.*

and Talbot, and Morton and Evandale. In *Rob Roy* the ideal is
best exemplified by Rob and the Bailie :

> After kissing each other very lovingly, and when they
> were just in the act of parting, the Bailie, in the fulness
> of his heart, and with a faltering voice, assured his kins-
> man, " that if ever an hundred pund, or even twa hundred,
> would put him or his family in a settled way, he need
> but just send a line to the Saut Market " ; and Rob,
> grasping his basket-hilt with one hand and shaking Mr
> Jarvie's heartily with the other, protested, " that if ever
> any body should affront his kinsman, an he would but
> let him ken, he would stow his lugs out of his head, were
> he the best man in Glasgow." [21]

Clan law applies everywhere, however, and it is the Bailie
who inherits from the MacVittie firm the Osbaldistone account
in Glasgow.

The principle of honour and reciprocity not only links
London with the Highlands, it also resolves the antithesis between the world of calculation and the world of heroism—the
figures of arithmetic and the figures of heraldry. This antithesis
finds its canniest expression in the gnomic rhetoric of Bailie
Nicol Jarvie. One of his speeches to Frank is interesting in that
it reveals quite casually how major issues in *Rob Roy* tend to
cluster around the question of filial obedience, but it is the sharpness of the antithesis that matters here :

> " Upon all these matters I am now to ask your advice,
> Mr Jarvie, which, I have no doubt, will point out the
> best way to act for my father's advantage and my own
> honour."
>
> " Ye're right, young man—ye're right," said the Bailie.
> " Aye take the counsel of those who are aulder and wiser
> than yoursell, and binna like the godless Rehoboam, who
> took the advice o' a wheen beardless callants, neglecting
> the old counsellors who had sate at the feet o' his father
> Solomon, and, as it was weel put by Mr Meiklejohn in his

[21] *R.R.*, ch. 36.

lecture on the chapter, were doubtless partakers of his sapience. But I maun hear naething about honour ; we ken naething here but about credit. Honour is a homicide and a bloodspiller, that gangs about making frays in the street ; but Credit is a decent honest man, that sits at hame and makes the pat play." [22]

The Bailie's last sentence is treasurable, but the example of William Osbaldistone proves it inadequate. Credit to him is simply honour by another name, and it can draw upon ancient and venerable states of feeling. It is no accident that both he and Rob Roy are gallant supporters of their respective sovereigns. Rob's devotion to the Stuarts is among his unsullied traits,[23] and on the other side we are reminded that just as the Elizabethan merchants helped to thwart the Armada by their manipulations, so their modern descendants, among whom William is very prominent, defend the Hanovers by buying up Government stock and saving the régime from bankruptcy.[24]

I do not detect irony in these similarities between William Osbaldistone and a Highland outlaw, nor do I sense any disapproval in Frank's reference to his father's " ardent spirit of enterprise and speculation." [25] It is worth observing, however, that William's interest is in speculation, not manufacture. *Ennui* must be avoided at all costs, and " trade has all the fascination of gambling without its moral guilt." [26] Here we observe one of Scott's most characteristic impulses. He would have derived great enjoyment from a career on Wall Street during its palmier days of unchecked marginal risk-taking. It is one of the ironies of literary history that *Rob Roy*, with its emphasis upon the pleasures of speculation and the necessity of commercial honour, should so accurately embody the system of values by which Scott lived and wrote and by which he was both to flounder into disaster in 1826 and to redeem himself.[27]

---

[22] *R.R.*, ch. 26. [23] *R.R.*, ch. 25. [24] *R.R.*, chs. 26. 37.
[25] *R.R.*, ch. 1. [26] *Ibid.*
[27] For a good discussion of the connexion of *Rob Roy* with Scott's own speculative practices as an author, see Grierson, *Sir Walter Scott, Bart.*, pp. 158-60.

The system of analogies and correspondences centred in the theme of fathers and sons, as well as the persistence and importance of the *motif* of honour, help to give order and unity to a novel that might have become a mere picaresque ramble against romantic backgrounds. Where *Rob Roy* breaks down, as we might expect, is in the ending. After the chastened and remorseful Frank has returned to the arms of his father he serves for a while in the loyal army against the Jacobite rebels, thus manifesting his adherence to proper authority. Significantly, we are told of Frank's military service in the same paragraph that describes his father's financial services to the same government.[28] Nevertheless, just as the trajectory of the plot seems to move in the direction of an inevitable and total unity of effort between father and son, Scott's devil takes control and deflects his hero to Northumberland and the life of the landed gentleman. This time we have none of the questionable manipulations that characterise the last chapters of *Old Mortality*. Instead Scott, with culpable contempt for his medium, kills off five sons of Sir Hildebrand on one page.[29] We hear no more of Frank's serving his father in business. Nor does Scott's wilfulness stop here. Although the political and religious differences between Frank and Diana are as wide as ever, and although she has bidden him a final and absolute farewell no less than four times,[30] Frank marries her just the same. Thus the Prodigal Son returns, only to be sent off again with his father's blessing and allowed to settle down with his whimsical and " improper " wife in Northumberland, not too far from the Highland haunts of riotous living. With the exception of the character of the heroine, it is the *Waverley* compromise all over again.

The plot of *Rob Roy* is flawed, but not irredeemably, and in the area of characterisation Scott achieves some notable successes. Rob Roy himself is convincing as long as we pass by Scott's linguistic problems and allow him to turn Rob into a Lowlander with no more Gaelic than the very little Scott could muster. Andrew Fairservice is Scott's saltiest manservant—a proud

---

[28] *R.R.*, ch. 27.   [29] *R.R.*, ch. 37.
[30] See *R.R.*, chs. 17, 33, 35, 39.

Scot whose mingled greed, fidelity, hypocrisy, and conceit are handled as though such a mixture of traits were no problem whatsoever. When forced to admit that he has been a smuggler in his day, Andrew exhibits a fine combination of self-righteousness and local feeling:

> " It's a mere spoiling o' the Egyptians. . . . Puir auld Scotland suffers eneugh by thae blackguard loons o' excisemen and gaugers, that hae come down on her like locusts since the sad and sorrowfu' Union ; it's the part of a kind son to bring her a soup o' something that will keep up her auld heart, and that will they nill they, the ill-fa'ard thieves." [31]

But the triumph of the novel is Bailie Nicol Jarvie, who is so fully alive that he very nearly runs away with the story. The Bailie is interesting as a mediating figure between Lowland and Highlands.[32] His analysis of the Highland situation is actually a sophisticated essay in social history and economic determinism. At times, especially when dealing with the fates of individuals, it rises to something like poetry:

> " But the times cam hard, and Rob was venturesome. It wasna my faut—it wasna my faut ; he canna wyte me. I aye tauld him o't. And the creditors, mair especially some grit neighbours o' his, grippit to his living and land ; and they say his wife was turned out o' the house to the hillside, and sair misguided to the boot. Shamefu'! shamefu'! I am a peacefu' man and a magistrate, but if ony ane had guided sae muckle as my servant quean, Mattie, as it's like they guided Rob's wife, I think it suld hae set the shabble that my father the deacon had at Bothwell Brig a-walking again. Well, Rob cam hame, and fand desolation, God pity us ! where he left plenty ; he looked east, west, south, north, and saw neither hauld

---

[31] *R.R.*, ch. 18.

[32] David Daiches, " Scott's Achievement as a Novelist ", in *Literary Essays*, Edinburgh 1956, p. 11.

nor hope—neither beild nor shelter ; sae he e'en pu'd the
bonnet ower his brow, belted the broadsword to his side,
took to the brae-side, and became a broken man." [33]

One of the reasons for the success of such passages as this is
that the Bailie's compassion is without the sentimentality that
ruins so much of the fictional treatment of the unfortunate in the
literature of Scott's day. Just how unsentimental Scott can be is
shown by the author's comment on the Bailie's speech :

> The voice of the good citizen was broken by his
> contending feelings. He obviously, while he professed
> to condemn the pedigree of his Highland kinsman,
> attached a secret feeling of consequence to the
> connexion. . . . [34]

It is in part the Bailie's " secret feeling of consequence " that
converts him into a comic Quixote, journeying into the Highlands with Frank only to confront, in the bloodstained Helen
MacGregor, an ancestral rage too intense to be encompassed by
his understanding of the Highlands, however deep. Exposed
to the spectacle of her ruthlessness, the Bailie seems rather pitiful,
and of all the characters of *Rob Roy* he is the happiest to return
to his city.[35] One of the shrewder touches of the novel occurs
after his return, when he marries his " servant quean " Mattie.
The marriage is a surprise, since it involves an elevation in
Maggie's status, and we are told that the Bailie was ridiculed for
it.[36] But the Bailie has referred to her often enough for the
reader to understand that she is one of the reference points of his
world. His linking of Maggie's name with Helen MacGregor's
in the speech quoted above, while it certainly relegates Maggie
to an inferior role in the analogy. nevertheless places her in the
position of a consort. Besides, as the Bailie says, " Mattie was
nae ordinary lassock quean ; she was akin to the Laird o' Limmer-
field." [37]

Scott's hand was never surer than in its management of the

---

[33] *R.R.*, ch. 26. [34] *Ibid.* [35] *R.R.*, ch. 36.
[36] *Ibid.* [37] *Ibid.*

Bailie. The two central characters, however, are more of a problem. There can be no question that Diana Vernon is an exhilarating change from Scott's previous polite heroines. Her first appearance, as she rides to hounds with the Osbaldistones, tells a great deal about her :

> It was a young lady, the loveliness of whose very striking features was enhanced by the animation of the chase and the glow of the exercise, mounted on a beautiful horse, jet black, unless where he was flecked by spots of the snow-white foam which embossed his bridle. She wore, what was then somewhat unusual, a coat, vest, and hat resembling those of a man, which fashion has since called a riding-habit. . . . Her long black hair streamed on the breeze, having in the hurry of the chase escaped from the ribbon which bound it.[38]

This is one of Scott's most well-managed entrances, preparing the reader for the sheer novelty of the character as it is to be developed. Nevertheless, Francis Jeffrey may have hit the mark when he called Diana " rather a more violent fiction . . . than a king with marble legs." [39] The trouble is that Die is simply too much—a devout Catholic, a self-sacrificing daughter, an active Jacobite, an ambitious bluestocking, a transvestite, a huntress, a romantic social critic—an amalgam, in short, of Flora MacIvor, Mary Wortley Montagu, and Buffalo Bill. Perhaps because there is so much in her requiring expression, her volubility is overwhelming. It is also hyper-masculine. Andrew Lang, one of her warmest admirers, found her " loving and . . . light of heart " and likened her to Rosalind.[40] What, then, are we to make of the following ?

> " So you may see Jobson on such occasions, like a bit of a broken-down blood-tit condemned to drag an over-loaded cart, puffing, strutting, and spluttering to get the

[38] *R.R.*, ch. 5.

[39] *Edinburgh Review*, LVIII (1818), p. 410.

[40] A. Lang, Editor's Introduction to *Rob Roy*, Border Edition, London, 1883, p. xvii.

Justice put in motion, while, though the wheels groan, creak, and revolve slowly, the great and preponderating weight of the vehicle fairly frustrates the efforts of the willing quadruped, and prevents its being brought into a state of actual progression." [41]

Thus she concludes a single unbroken utterance of over 600 words. Scott himself might have become exhausted, for after Frank leaves for Scotland Die drops away and becomes a distant focus of affection, reappearing only briefly as a nightrider in the Highlands.[42] When they meet later she appears with " diminished beauty and sunk spirits " and an " air of composed and submissive but dauntless resolution and constancy." [43] She is ready for marriage at last.

That she marries Frank might strike some readers as unfitting. Frank is one of Scott's least attractive heroes, combining a bristling pride with unusual passivity. The passivity is most obvious when he sits looking out of a coach window while Rob Roy kills his worst enemy.[44] The pride emerges, not only as legitimate *motif* in the story, but also as an annoying tendency, shared to a degree by other Scott heroes, to stand upon his honour in the sulkiest fashion possible. Having offended his cousins by drinking himself into a rage the night before he apologises the next day like a prickly *petit-maître*. " No circumstances," he says to the offended Rashleigh, " could have wrung from me a single word of apology save my own consciousness of the impropriety of my behaviour." [45] Surely an author who knew his Shakespeare as well as Scott might have remembered Hamlet and Laertes.

Unsympathetic as he is, however, Frank provides two moments in *Rob Roy* that are both impassioned and melancholy. One of them occurs as he walks alone in the Highlands and is overtaken by Die and her father. The scene of the unexpected meeting is one of the most intense ever conceived by Scott, and Frank's response takes him into an entirely new realm of feeling :

[41] *R.R.*, ch. 7.   [42] *R.R.*, ch. 33.   [43] *R.R.*, ch. 38.
[44] *R.R.*, ch. 39.   [45] *R.R.*, ch. 12.

I remained motionless with the packet in my hand, gazing after them as if endeavouring to count the sparkles which flew from the horses' hoofs. I continued to look after even these had ceased to be visible, and to listen to their footsteps long after the last distant trampling had died in my ears. At length tears rushed to my eyes, glazed as they were by the exertion of straining after what was no longer to be seen. I wiped them mechanically, and almost without being aware that they were flowing, but they came thicker and thicker. I felt the tightening of the throat and breast, the *hysterica passio* of poor Lear; and, sitting down by the wayside, I shed a flood of the first and most bitter tears which had flowed from my eyes since childhood.[46]

The second passage is more modest and conventional. Returning to the emptiness of Osbaldistone Hall at the end of his Scottish adventures, Frank sits down in twilight before the fire and reflects on the waste of human ambition:

" And this," said I alone, " is the progress and the issue of human wishes ! Nursed by the merest trifles, they are first kindled by fancy, nay, are fed upon the vapour of hope till they consume the substance which they inflame ; and man, and his hopes, passions, and desires, sink into a worthless heap of embers and ashes ! " [47]

The language here is not of the best, but the feeling is genuine and important. We are in touch with an irreducible melancholy that looks back to Morton and ahead to Ravenswood. It is a feeling that should not be forgotten, even though in his next work Scott was to do without a hero altogether and carry his most engaging heroine through to a convincing success.

[46] *R.R.*, ch. 33.   [47] *R.R.*, ch. 38.

6

THE HEART OF MIDLOTHIAN

" D--n her, why must she needs speak the truth,
when she could have as well said anything else
she had a mind ? "

— *The Heart of Midlothian*, Ch. 34

The Heart of Midlothian is Scott's most ambitious novel. It exceeds *Waverley* and *Old Mortality* in breadth of scope and variety of characterization, and it dramatises a question of personal morality so crucial that the reader commonly loses all detachment and enters the novel as a judge.

Scott based the plot of his novel on the story of Helen Walker, which he summarises in his introduction. Helen was the legal guardian of a younger sister who was brought to trial for child-murder. The law under which she was tried assumed the defendant guilty unless she could be proven to have confessed her pregnancy. But Helen had heard no confession, and she refused to commit the beneficent perjury that would have procured her sister's acquittal. Determined, however, to frustrate the consequences of her own cruel honesty, she carried her sister's case to the Duke of Argyle in London, who obtained her sister's pardon.

Told in this bare fashion, the story of Helen Walker can be

accepted as an unusual instance of moral fortitude and providential success. When the story is given substance and detail, however, problems arise. The distant and almost legendary Helen becomes the morally anxious Jeanie Deans, and the unhappy sister becomes the immediate and believable Effie. At once the question may be asked: who is Jeanie Deans to condemn her sister to execution for the sake of her own sense of moral integrity? The comment of Effie's jailor, in a dramatisation of the novel witnessed by George Bernard Shaw, is understandable: " I wad ha sworn a hole through an iron pot." Shaw endorses the sentiment and expresses regret that Scott wasn't an Ibsen to expose Jeanie's underlying egotism and false idealism.[1]

This much can be conceded to Shaw—that Scott is on unfamiliar ground in *The Heart of Midlothian*. Jeanie Deans's problem is at once more private and more abstract than any he had handled previously. It has the flavour of a seminar in ethics, for it lends itself to academic discussions of the possible justifications of lying. Scott's practice in his previous novels had been to take the principles of personal morality as assumed. His heroes and heroines were automatically virtuous, resisting without effort the routine temptations of the world and the flesh. By leaving such waters untroubled Scott was able to concentrate on the problems arising from conflicts of loyalties in politically disturbed eras. Jeanie's conflict, however, is between her love for her sister and her love for truth, and she must solve the problem in isolation. Perhaps his unfamiliarity with such situations led Scott into the platitudinous writing of which Donald Davie and Joseph Warren Beach complained.[2] It must be admitted that Scott is excessively careful at times to exhibit the proper responses.

Nevertheless, *The Heart of Midlothian*, with the exception of its disastrous conclusion, is no failure, for Scott managed to solve

[1] G. Bernard Shaw, *The Quintessence of Ibsenism*, in *The Works of Bernard Shaw*, 33 vols., London 1930–8, XIX. 125.

[2] J. Warren Beach, *The Twentieth Century Novel : Studies in Technique*, New York 1932, pp. 17-18 ; Donald Davie, *The Heyday of Sir Walter Scott*, London 1961, pp. 13-15.

his problem by providing Jeanie's critical act of truth-telling with a social context that justifies her rigour by contrast. In other words, he sets the story of Helen Walker in a novel of political confusion and joins the edges as smoothly as he can. Hence the use that he makes of the Porteous riots. Scott's juxtaposition of this episode of civil rebellion with the story of Jeanie was in the strictest sense gratuitous. None of the connexions he so carefully makes between the rebellious Robertson-Staunton and the two sisters can fail to conceal the fact that Jeanie's dilemma would have arisen without the riots. What raises the Porteous episodes above the level of a *coup de théâtre*, however, is the effect they have upon men's ability to hear and speak the truth, and that, of course, is precisely what Effie's trial is all about. The riots were an act of defiance against England and the Union —a revolt coloured with every conceivable degree of bias and venality on both sides. Here Scott is in his element. The colouring of political thought by " interest," the murky character of popular indignation, the accessibility of all parties to rumour, the ease with which opposing factions adopt the therapy of group self-pity and the lies to justify it—these are phenomena that Scott knew as well as any writer before or since. The result is that the opening chapters of *The Heart of Midlothian* offer a definitive portrait of a world in which Truth is dead—even to the narrator.

Everywhere in these chapters facts are hard to come by, and, if discovered, are difficult to classify. The Porteous mob was indeed well-disciplined and acted with Mosaic precision in its concentration on Porteous alone.[3] But why was Porteous being lynched? For deliberately firing on the citizens of Edinburgh? The testimony is conflicting on this point, and Scott does little to clear it up.[4] He knows that Porteous is being killed for other reasons: his personal unpopularity, his identification with resented authority, his reported tolerance of debauchery, in short, for many grievances, "some real, and many imaginary."[5] Again, Wilson and Robertson are enemies of the law, but are they criminals? Yes and no, for theirs is the ambiguous crime of smuggling, which lies half-way between robbery for gain and

---

³ *H.M.*, ch. 7.   ⁴ *H.M.*, ch. 3.   ⁵ *Ibid.*

justified national self-assertion. Was the British Government right to pardon Porteous? Perhaps, but it was apparently acting in response to the urging of timid Edinburgh magistrates more concerned for their own safety and the approval of the British cabinet than for the achievement of justice.[6] And when the Queen explodes to Argyle in London about the Scots her passions are as cloudy and "interested" as those of the rioters.[7] Scott's narrative of these events has vividness and power, but his refusal to take sides discourages the partisan. C. M. Grieve, both intensely Scottish and intensely Marxist, could not forgive Scott for failing to glorify the riots as an inspiring national and proletarian act of defiance.[8] Right or wrong, Grieve's reaction deserves notice as a warning that the world of the Waverley Novels can be a frustrating place for passionate believers.

When Scott turns from the Porteous affair to the lives of the Deans and the Butlers, the atmosphere becomes more meditative and pastoral. But factional prejudice and doctrinaire inheritance can still convert good men into partisan automata. David Deans, by all outward and visible signs, is a good and virtuous man, and Scott handles him gently. Unfortunately he is also a descendant of the Covenanters, conscious of the historical defeat of his sect, and when he learns that Effie is pregnant it is the petulant doctrinaire who gets the upper hand. We may be accustomed to regarding sectarian feeling as a luxury to be abandoned in times of crisis. With Deans the opposite occurs, and the father is swallowed up in the Presbyterian. Effie is no erring daughter to be reclaimed by love, but a traitor who has let down the side:

> "But to be the father of a castaway, a profligate, a
> bloody Zipporah, a mere murderess! O, how will the
> wicked exult in the high places of their wickedness!—
> the prelatists, and the latitudinarians. . . ." [9]

Deans is sometimes a comic figure, but there is no mistaking the extent to which his sectarian passion has obliterated

---

[6] *H.M.*, ch. 4.   [7] *H.M.*, ch. 7.

[8] C. M. Grieve ("Hugh MacDiarmid"), *Lucky Poet*, London 1943, p. 207.   [9] *H.M.*, ch. 10.

charity; in his own way he is just as mindless and terrifying as the Porteous mob. Responding to the idiotic Saddletree's catalogue of advocates available to defend her, he eliminates all on ideological grounds as though Effie's fate was the least of his concerns:

> " Now, I could speak to Mr. Crossmyloof; he's weel kenn'd for a round-spun Presbyterian, and a ruling elder to boot."
> " He's a rank Yerastian," replied Deans. . . .
> " What say ye to the auld Laird of Cuffabout? " said Saddletree. . . .
> " He! the fause loon! " answered Deans. " He was in his bandaliers to hae joined the ungracious High-landers in 1715, an they had ever had the luck to cross the Firth."
> " Weel, Arniston? there's a clever chield for ye! " said Bartoline, triumphantly.
> " Ay, to bring popish medals in till their very library from that schismatic woman in the north, the Duchess of Gordon."
> " Weel, weel, but somebody ye maun hae. What think ye o' Kittlepunt? "
> " He's an Arminian."
> " Woodsetter? "
> " He's, I doubt, a Cocceian." [10]

Thus David Deans shares in the evil of Jeanie Deans's world. Many an eighteenth-century writer had denounced " the dogs of faction " in conventional terms. It remained for Scott to show that " faction " engages the depths of the personality and can lead to the death of truth and charity together.

Nowhere in the Waverley Novels is Scott's narrative style more suited to his subject than in the chapters leading up to the trial of Effie. Here we may observe a combination of influences— the scholarly caution of the judicious historians and editors Scott knew so well, the stylistic reticence of the legal report, above

[10] *H.M.*, ch. 12.

all, perhaps the ironically tentative manner of Fielding, who, by occasionally withholding narrative information, judges by implication those of his characters who are too quick to condemn his heroes on the basis of gossip. Alexander Welsh, in his discussion of Scott's " tentative fiction," comments on the element of imprecision in Scott's narrative vocabulary and finds its cause in Scott's commitment to the writing of romance rather than tragedy and in his inward obeisance to the abstract relationships of a property-centred society. I am too indebted to Welsh's shrewdness and sensitivity to do more than point out that in *The Heart of Midlothian* Scott's vagueness serves both a critical and a revelatory purpose. In response to Ruskin's vehement complaint about Scott's " incapacity of steady belief in anything "—an opinion for which Welsh seems to have some sympathy—we may ask, " Who is omniscient in a world where truth is dead ? " [11] Certainly not Scott's *persona*, Jedediah Cleishbotham, whose stance is very similar to that of a court reporter, imprisoned in a situation in which the truth is something that happened at a distance and on another day—something that must be discovered by balancing interest against interest and holding all testimony in doubt. Hence we get paragraphs like the following, in which Scott marshals his defensive qualifications in a description of the Edinburgh mob.

> The assembled spectators of almost all degrees, whose minds had been wound up to the pitch which we have described, uttered a groan, *or rather a roar* of indignation and disappointed revenge, similar to that of a tiger from whom his meal has been rent by his keeper when he was just about to devour it. This fierce exclamation *seemed to forebode* some immediate explosion of popular resentment, and, in fact, such had been expected by the magistrates, and the necessary measures had been taken to repress it. But the shout was not repeated, nor did any sudden

[11] John Ruskin, *Modern Painters, in The Works of John Ruskin,* edd. E. T. Cook and A. Wedderburn, London 1902–12, v. 336. Also see Welsh, *The Hero of the Waverley Novels,* pp. 189–98.

G

tumult ensue, such as *it appeared to announce.* The populace *seemed to be ashamed* of having expressed their disappointment in a vain clamour, and the sound changed, not into the silence which had preceded the arrival of these stunning news, but into stifled mutterings. . . .[12]

Or this, in which an incident is half believed :

No opposition was offered to their entrance, either by the guards or doorkeepers ; and it is even said that one of the latter refused a shilling of civility-money, tendered him by the Laird of Dumbiedykes, who was of opinion that " siller wad mak a' easy." But this last incident wants confirmation.[13]

Or this, on the question of Porteous's guilt :

After a long and patient hearing, the jury had the difficult duty of balancing the positive evidence of many persons, and those of respectability, who deposed positively to the prisoner's commanding his soldiers to fire, and himself firing his piece, of which some swore that they saw the smoke and flash, and beheld a man drop at whom it was pointed, with the negative testimony of others, who, though well stationed for seeing what had passed, neither heard Porteous give orders to fire, nor saw him fire himself ; but, on the contrary, averred that the first shot was fired by a soldier who stood close by him. A great part of his defence was also founded on the turbulence of the mob, which witnesses, according to their feelings, their predilections, and their opportunities of observation, represented differently ; some describing as a formidable riot what others represented as a trifling disturbance, such as always used to take place on the like occasions, when the executioner of the law and the men commissioned to protect him in his task were generally exposed to some indignities.[14]

[12] *H.M.*, ch. 4 ; my italics.   [13] *H.M.*, ch. 21.   [14] *H.M.*, ch. 3.

Such a style implies an explicit criticism of those characters in the novel who are dogmatic and self-assured, whether pathetic doctrinaires like David Deans or impenetrable fools like Bartoline Saddletree. It also provides a properly ironic framework for the law under which Effie is condemned. This law, unlike the narrator himself, presumes certainty where there is none, paradoxically interpreting non-communication as an admission of guilt. Only some rather orotund language can do justice to such a statute, and Scott gives it to the prosecuting counsel, whose meaning is removed to a further distance by Scott's use of indirect discourse :

> It was not, however, necessary for him to bring positive proof that the panel was accessory to the murder, nay, nor even to prove that the child was murdered at all. It was sufficient to support the indictment, that it could not be found. According to the stern but necessary severity of this statute, she who should conceal her pregnancy, who should omit to call that assistance which is most necessary on such occasions, was held already to have meditated the death of her offspring, as an event most likely to be the consequence of her culpable and cruel concealment.[15]

There is a suggestion of logic in the law as summarised in this way, but it is a logic based upon the eighteenth-century view of " nature " at its worst—presumptuous, authoritarian, and contemptuous of particulars. It is a law, as Jeanie indicates to Argyle, that is itself a murderer.[16] Moreover, Scott will not allow this statute immunity from the general contagion of petulant nationalism, for Argyle points out that it is maintained in part by " the prejudice in government against the Scottish nation at large." [17]

Another consequence of Scott's indecisive style is the longing it creates in the attentive reader for someone—almost anyone at all—to stand up and speak the unadorned truth whatever his bias may be. Thus style operates in quiet ways to justify Jeanie's

[15] *H.M.*, ch. 22.   [16] *H.M.*, ch. 35.   [17] *Ibid.*

testimony in court. Moreover, our appetite for truth can be
satisfied in one way only. Given the character of Jeanie's world,
in which truth is so persistently deflected by interest, the only
visible sign of Jeanie's honesty will lie in the consequence of her
testimony. It *must* go against the grain. Her wretchedness at
the trial is our guarantee of the validity of what she says. Scott
makes her dilemma all the more painful by having Effie's advocate
struggle right up to the last moment to induce perjury :

> "Take courage, young woman," said Fairbrother.
> "I asked what your sister said ailed her when you
> inquired ? "
> "Nothing," answered Jeanie, with a faint voice, which
> was yet heard distinctly in the most distant corner of the
> courtroom. . . .
> Fairbrother's countenance fell ; but with that ready
> presence of mind which is as useful in civil as in military
> emergencies, he immediately rallied. "Nothing ? True ;
> you mean nothing at *first* ; but when you asked her again,
> did she not tell you what ailed her ? "
> The question was put in a tone meant to make her
> comprehend the importance of her answer, had she not
> been already aware of it. The ice was broken, however,
> and with less pause than at first, she now replied—
> "Alack ! alack ! she never breathed word to me about it." [18]

The effect of this passage is complex. Jeanie's "Nothing,"
like Cordelia's, is a clear light in a world of lies, yet it leads to a
sentence of death for Effie. Scott is interested here in the tension
between the claims of the real and the ideal that is one of the
tragic facts of human life. We can only be grateful that he was
not an Ibsen. To "expose" Jeanie as a self-deceiving egoist
would have been to drag her back into the world of venality over
which she so miserably triumphs. It would be to eliminate
Scott's moral tension and substitute for it the crude over-
simplifications of one more psychological doctrinaire case-
history.

[18] *H.M.*, ch. 23.

What follows Jeanie's testimony is her attempt to find in the British world an institutional counterpart of her own transcendent moral impulse. Hence her journey to the Queen, whose royal prerogative gives her unimpeachable powers over the corruptions and injustices of the realm. Scott knows that a just society is one in which the telling of a truth does not lead to unjust consequences. The child-murder law is obviously unjust by this standard. Hence the force of the proverbial saying that hovers in Jeanie's mind: "The King's face, that gives Grace." Because the law itself is coloured by human passion and prejudice, there must be in the realm the secular image of a divine gift, capable at critical times of cutting the knot of injustice and rescuing honesty from the clutches of subtle lawyers and vindictive partisans. This quasi-divine role of royalty is underscored by Scott in his heading for Chapter 37: "You are a God above us ;/Be as a God, then, full of saving mercy!"

And so Jeanie goes to Queen Caroline, and there one vessel of grace confronts another, and justice is done. It is to Scott's credit that the scene between Jeanie and the Queen comes off so well. Scott here reveals his capacity to succeed with ease in situations that would baffle lesser talents. The verbal problems arising out of the confrontation between the language of the barnyard and the rural conventicle and the language of the court are solved by holding Jeanie's dialect within bounds and, on the other hand, allowing her only the simplest of abstractions:

O, madam, if ever you kenn'd what it was to sorrow for
and with a sinning and a suffering creature, whose mind
is sae tossed that she can be neither ca'd fit to live or
die, have some compassion on our misery! Save an honest
house from dishonour, and an unhappy girl, not eighteen
years of age, from an early and dreadful death! Alas!
it is not when we sleep soft and wake merrily ourselves,
that we think on other people's sufferings. Our hearts
are waxed light within us then, and we are for righting
our ain wrangs and fighting our ain battles. But when the
hour of trouble comes to the mind or to the body—and

seldom may it visit your Leddyship—and when the hour
of death comes, that comes to high and low—lang and
late may it be yours—O, my Leddy, then it isna what we
hae dune for oursells, but what we hae dune for others,
that we think on maist pleasantly. And the thoughts that
ye hae intervened to spare the puir thing's life will be
sweeter in that hour, come when it may, than if a word
of your mouth could hang the haill Porteous mob at the
tail of ae tow.[19]

Jeanie is asserting truth and justice in the midst of a storm of
ill-will between two countries. Her style may please Scot or
Sassenach no more than " *franglais* " pleases De Gaulle or the
French Academy, but its mixed character is dramatically relevant
to her purpose. Moreover, Scott, resolved that Jeanie shall
remain in keeping, sees that her human limitations are not
forgotten. She needs Argyle's help, and in her talk of tartans
and cheeses practices upon him with instinctive cunning. But
before the Queen her habitual concreteness leads her to babble
on about family virtues without realising that some of her remarks apply to court scandals in a potentially disastrous way.

As for the Queen, who in the actual outcome of the novel is
just as necessary a figure as Jeanie, Scott keeps her properly in
her place by making it clear that while Jeanie's strength lies in her
character, hers comes from her station. Her previously expressed anger at the Scots shows her capacity for nationalistic
passion. When Jeanie's speech is finished, she remains affected,
but detached. " This is eloquence," she remarks, as one might
judge a school forensic contest, and when Jeanie leaves she gives
her a fifty-pound note and—a needle case !

It is only after Jeanie's triumphant interview that the novel
fades. What follows is a disaster which reveals perhaps as nothing else in the Waverley Novels Scott's capacity for an infantile
disregard of aesthetic decencies. *The Heart of Midlothian* concludes its third volume with Jeanie's royal interview. What
follows is enough matter to fill the fourth volume that his con-

<hr>

[19] *H.M.*, ch. 37.

tract called for. Whatever efforts can be made to discover thematic validity in the concluding chapters,[20] they remain a sad and boring affair, full of irrelevant characters and a totally unrecognisable Effie (now Lady Staunton), and garnished with an excess of melodrama and false morality. Dorothy Van Ghent has forbiddingly reminded us that the task of revising novels belongs to the novelist,[21] but we may be forgiven for wanting to close with the end of the third volume, when Jeanie, her mission accomplished, walks away from the Queen's presence.

The difficulty is that even if Scott had let his novel stand there, the ending would be wrong. His arrangement of volumes—which remained constant from the manuscript stage through the first printing—allows for no satisfactory conclusion. Scott could hardly have ended with Vol. III as it now stands. Such a conclusion would be wretchedly abrupt, denying us the pleasure of the cadential distribution of characters that is one of the chief formal a delights of the popular novel of tradition. If we must imagine a better ending, only one possibility emerges. The final scene should be the reunion scene between Jeanie and the chastened David, now in Ch. 42, followed by the wedding of Jeanie and Reuben Butler. But such satisfactions exist only in the realm of lost chances, and the reader had best soldier on until Scott has finally met his quota.

Eventually, of course, Jeanie and Reuben survive the melodrama of the last chapters and continue their lives in pastoral happiness. The impression remains that some sort of miracle has occurred. In the atmosphere of the novel Jeanie's victory is as rare as her truth-telling. Never before in the Waverley Novels—except, perhaps, in the comic dissociations of *The Antiquary*—have the times been so completely out of joint. In *Old Mortality* the State returns to order, but the principals do not. In *The Heart of Midlothian* the wreck of individuals echoes the chaos in society. As David Daiches has indicated, history is the enemy, depriving men and nations of their characters and

[20] See David Daiches, Introduction to *The Heart of Midlothian*, New York 1948, pp. xii-xiii.
[21] D. Van Ghent, *The English Novel*, pp. 114-15.

functions.[22] The rebelliousness of Scotland against England finds its parallel in the rebellion of Staunton against his father—and in each case what is lost is no abstract liberty but a style of life. Robertson was a born soldier who satisfied his thirst for action by smuggling, just as Scotland, no longer sending armies into the field against England, resorts to rioting and lynching. Other characters echo these patterns. Madge Wildfire resembles Meg Merrilies in her appearance and wandering habits,[23] but Madge, unlike Meg, is an ineffectual, though charming, madwoman. (Interestingly, the late eighteenth-century setting of *Guy Mannering*, in which Meg achieves so much, offered less scope for a gypsy than the late 1730s, but Scott's darkening view of historical process is the controlling element, not the knowledge of events he would have had as a social historian.) Young Dumbiedykes is interesting as a comically extreme example of a loss of strength and individuality that shows itself everywhere. His father, who " soughed awa'...in an attempt to sing ' Deil stick the minister,' " is tough, greedy, and at peace with himself. Only in his death scene—one of the finest in the British novel—does he express his fear of Hell, " in a tone which made the very attorney shudder," but he dies obdurate.[24] As for his gaping son, his famous farewell to Jeanie as she is setting out for London says all that is needful :

> Dumbiedykes turned and waved his hand ; and his pony, much more willing to return than he had been to set out, hurried him homewards so fast that, wanting the aid of a regular bridle, as well as of saddle and stirrups, he was too much puzzled to keep his seat to permit of his looking behind, even to give the parting glance of a forlorn swain. I am ashamed to say that the sight of a lover, run away with in nightgown and slippers and a laced hat, by a bare-backed Highland pony, had something in it of a sedative, even to a grateful and deserved burst of affectionate esteem. The figure of Dumbiedykes was too ludicrous

[22] David Daiches, introduction to *H.M.*, pp. vii-xi.
[23] *H.M.*, ch. 16.   [24] *H.M.*, ch. 8.

not to confirm Jeanie in the original sentiments she
entertained towards him.

" He's a gude creature," said she, " and a kind ; it's a
pity he has sae willyard a powny." [25]

Even Reuben Butler, the grandson of a vigorous and colourful
Cromwellian soldier, is constitutionally sickly, and he benefits
from the more " masculine " guidance of Jeanie.[26]

Thus *The Heart of Midlothian* is distinguished by the persistence with which it exploits the pathos of family discontinuance.
The strength of the fathers is not available to the children.
Staunton's father can offer his errant son nothing but conven-
tionally pious rebuke, and it is Jeanie who dominates the vapor-
ous exchange between them.[27] The fitting conclusion to the
Staunton story is the fate of the younger Staunton's son, who is
last heard of going native among the American Indians.[28]
Nothing could be in sharper contrast to *Rob Roy*, with its series
of firm father-son relationships and its warm reconciliation scene
between the two Osbaldistones. The reunion between Jeanie
and David Deans after her return from London is actually a
reversal of the *Rob Roy* reunion, for it is the child who here
receives the homage of the parent whose ineffectual rigour would
have lost Effie for ever.[29]

Except for Jeanie's intense loyalty, the family situations in
The Heart of Midlothian are emblems of a widespread social
breakdown. It is a far more terrifying breakdown than any Scott
had shown before, for it involves both the fragmentation of the
contemporary social order and the loss of continuity between
one generation and another. In such a thoroughly disrupted
world Jeanie's strength would have been of no avail were it not
for the existence of one supremely privileged person—the
Queen. Thus, despite its concluding discourse on the power of
Providence, *The Heart of Midlothian* marks the appearance in
the Waverley Novels of a deeply felt, almost desperate, royalism.

[25] *H.M.*, ch. 26.   [26] *H.M.*, ch. 9.   [27] *H.M.*, ch. 34.
[28] *H.M.*, ch. 52.   [29] *H.M.*, ch. 42.

7

THE BRIDE
OF LAMMERMOOR

" Life could not be endured were it seen in
reality."

— Scott's *Journal*

The tragic climax of Scott's series of Scottish novels occurs in
The Bride of Lammermoor. Originally intended as a companion
piece to *The Heart of Midlothian,* it carries all the gloomier
implications of that work to a logical conclusion, and it does so
with a simplicity of line and a unity of style that make it the most
artistically effective of the Scottish novels.

Superficially *The Bride* appears anti-realistic. Its Gothicism,
its witches, its tragic story of love thwarted by a society villain-
ness, its conclusion in madness and death, are matters of which
ballads are made. Having witnessed the ubiquity of Scott's
political, interests, however we know better than to assume that
The Bride is a working over of romantic material for its own sake.
We are not surprised to observe that the ferocious Lady Ashton,
who frustrates the two lovers, is a Whig thriving on " new
money " and out for Tory blood, that Scotland's loss of her
throne contributes to the hero's disaster, and that Edgar and Lucy,
the star-crossed lovers, are given to debating the relative merits

of the Kirk and " the prelatical form of church government." [1]

The real novelty of *The Bride* is that its conservative bias, while not unqualified, is more emphatic than that of any of its predecessors, with the possible and harmless exception of *Guy Mannering*. Edgar Ravenswood is the descendant of an ancient line of feudal predators, but their power has vanished. Doubtless their " pride and turbulence "[2] had much to do with their decline, but there were other causes as well. Edgar's father had chosen the wrong side in 1689 and had fallen victim to the political influence of Sir William Ashton, " a skilful fisher in the troubled waters of a state divided by factions." [3] Ashton had engaged the elder Ravenswood in a series of lawsuits over the title to Ravenswood Castle. Scott implies that Ashton's membership and influence in the dominant Whig party had much to do with his ultimate legal victory—a victory that resulted in the eviction of the Ravenswoods from their castle to a mouldering fortress overlooking the North Sea.[4] But Ashton's triumph is almost guaranteed by the decadent state of the realm :

> " In those days there was no king in Israel." . . . There was no supreme power, claiming and possessing a general interest with the community at large, to whom the oppressed might appeal from subordinate tyranny, either for justice or for mercy. Let a monarch be as indolent, as selfish, as much disposed to arbitrary power as he will, still, in a free country, his own interests are so clearly connected with those of the public at large . . . that common policy, as well as common feeling, point to the equal distribution of justice, and to the establishment of the throne in righteousness.[5]

The Scottish legal system is in decay :

> The administration of justice . . . was infected by the most gross partiality. A case of importance scarcely occurred in which there was not some ground for bias

---

[1] *B.L.*, ch. 21.   [2] *B.L.*, ch. 2.   [3] *Ibid.*
         [4] *Ibid.*   [5] *Ibid.*

or partiality on the part of the judges, who were so little able to withstand the temptation that the adage, " Show me the man, and I will show you the law," became as prevalent as it was scandalous.[6]

This is an intensification of the dark social vision of *The Heart of Midlothian*, and there is nothing ambiguous about its Tory pessimism. The realm is in a condition of social disintegration, and its symptoms are the decline of ancient families, the corruption of justice, and a vicious factionalism.

Edgar Ravenswood is in love with Lucy Ashton. His love is absolute, therefore the continuance of his name and family will depend upon the success of his suit. His situation as a dedicated lover inevitably brings into operation that sympathy for honest suitors that is implied in the unwritten contract between the author of romantic fiction and his readers. But if the obstacles to Edgar are social and political rather than narrowly circumstantial, then he will obtain our sympathy as a decent victim of social evils.

That he is such a victim is made clear in his relations with three of the novel's most important characters: Sir William Ashton, Lady Ashton, and the Marquis of A———. Sir William and the Marquis are both political opportunists. Although the former is a Whig and the latter a Tory, they have in common a cynical tendency to adjust ideological principles to the prevailing political winds that documents the assault on factionalism in the second chapter. The Marquis has embraced Edgar's quarrel with the Ashtons over the Ravenswood estate in order to blackmail political support from Sir William, and Sir William desires friendship with Edgar should the Marquis and his fellow Tories win their struggle for power.[7] Edgar, of course, must be able to offer Lucy something better than a life of poverty with an outcast nobleman; therefore he enters into political partnership with the Marquis. His fortunes soon begin to follow a pattern dictated by the vicissitudes of party warfare. The inactivity with which he has been cursed finally ends when the Tories,

[6] *B.L.*, ch .2.   [7] *B.L.*, ch. 15.

guided by the Marquis, come to power, [8] Although he is no time-server or party strategist he becomes inextricably involved in their sordid intrigues. However, the reason for this touching of pitch is inescapable—he has nowhere else to go and no other way of fighting. History itself has snatched away his weapons.

Actually Edgar is incapable of taking an aggressive role in political conflicts. He exhibits an old-fashioned loyalty to the land that has nothing to do with partisan warfare, and like many a fictional victim of society he falls into bad company because he cannot help it. Scott shows us the world to which Edgar properly belongs by repeatedly associating him with the manners and rituals of the past: the outlawed Anglican funeral ceremony,[9] the Christian tradition of almsgiving,[10] the secular ritual of the chase.[11] It is to " our old Scottish days " that Edgar appeals in protesting against the cruelties of Sir William,[12] and it is Edgar's connexion with feudal antiquity that his servant Caleb invokes, when, trying to obtain food for Edgar's depleted pantry from the reluctant David Dingwall, he makes use of arguments arising from " antique custom and hereditary respect, from the good deeds done by the Lords of Ravenswood . . . in former days, and from what might be expected from them in future." [13] Doubtless Edgar's hatred of that same factionalism upon which he must now depend [14] is a reflexion of his link with the past. Ideally, Edgar is a purified remnant of another age, like Meg Merrilies in this respect, if in no other.

Both Sir William and the Marquis, on the other hand, are shrewd and dangerous moral nullities. Throughout the novel each of them exhibits an almost pathological inability to speak plainly. Sir William is a Glossin of national importance who turns Ravenswood Castle into a *parvenu's* project of self-advertisement,[15] while the Marquis is his image on the other side—an opportunistic Tory who enjoys hinting at his supposed Jacobite leanings as though participating in a fashionable affectation.[16]

Edgar's chief antagonist, however, is Lady Ashton. Beside

---

[8] *B.L.*, ch. 27. [9] *B.L.*, ch. 2. [10] *B.L.*, ch. 24.
[11] *B.L.*, ch. 9. [12] *B.L.*, ch. 7. [13] *B.L.*, ch. 12.
[14] *B.L.*, ch. 8. [15] *B.L.*, ch. 18. [16] *B.L.*, ch. 24.

this woman, one of Scott's successful examples of a type he always found difficult, the upper-class villain, Edgar appears noble indeed. She may have a sense of family pride that resembles his, but there the similarity ends. Her world is the world of party intrigue and treachery. Like her husband, she fishes in the waters of faction, for her political ambitions are boundless. She is a friend of the Duchess of Marlborough and similar in character to that formidable woman.[17]   Naturally she resents Edgar's efforts to regain his estate, yet Scott suggests that her enmity has other roots—that it arises from an aggregation of political, religious, and economic prejudices that document his description of Scotland as a society torn by internal divisions. As we would expect, she hates his politics, but she also finds religious sanctions for her hostility. Her letter to Edgar in Edinburgh employs the sulphurous polemical style of the Scottish Covenanters, and she denounces him because his family fought against " the immunities of God's kirk." [18]   She also rejects him because he is poor, denouncing hit as " a beggarly Jacobite bankrupt," [19] and hating him, according to the Marquis of A——, " for not having the lands that her goodman has." [20]   Her own spiritual guide, Peter Bide-the-Bent, has a text to support her : " The seed of the righteous are not seen begging their bread." [21]   Such attitudes as these demonstrate that Edgar Ravenswood dies in the Kelpie's Flow partly because of decadent Calvinism and what R. H. Tawney called " the triumph of the economic virtues." [22]

The fortunes of Edgar and our opinion of him as a person are certainly affected by the condition of Scotland as revealed in political intrigue and class hatreds. But if Edgar is the victim of historical circumstances, so is his irrepressible servant Caleb. Caleb is driven by the desire to keep up appearances. There is no foolish trickery to which he will not resort in order to conceal Edgar's poverty from the world. He wrecks Edgar's kitchen and pretends that a bolt of lightning did the damage, so that

---

[17] *B.L.*, ch. 15.   [18] *B.L.*, ch. 27.   [19] *B.L.*, ch. 22.
[20] *B.L.*, ch. 24.   [21] *B.L.*, ch. 13.
[22] R. H. Tawney, *Religion and the Rise of Capitalism : A Historical Study*, New York 1926, pp. 227-53.

Edgar may have an excuse for not serving his guests a decent dinner;[23] he steals a goose from a well-to-do citizen of the village of Wolf's Hope to piece out the imperfections of Edgar's pantry;[24] and he sets fire to the straw in the courtyard of Wolf's Crag to frighten away possible visitors, lest they see Edgar's fortress in its true drabness.[25]

Obviously Scott carried Caleb's monomania too far. He himself confessed that " he might have sprinkled rather too much parsley over his chicken." [26] But there is pathos in Caleb's desperation. He is made miserable, like Edgar, by his anachronistic role in society, for he may be described as the withered remnant of a once lordly aristocratic tradition. Scott shows that in the very act of stealing a goose Caleb acts from motives far more creditable than those that habitually govern the villagers. Caleb exhibits the virtue of loyalty, and this virtue shines all the more brightly when seen against the background of surly self-seeking that makes the village of Wolf's Hope a centre of moral paralysis. There the new Scotland has defeated the old. The townsfolk, who were once serfs of the Ravenswoods, have achieved independence, and their community has become a microcosm of the state; once again there is no king in Israel. The result is a formidable prefiguration of Faulkner's Snopes clan. The moral effects of " progress " are seen in Caleb's conversation with David Dingwall, a " country attorney " who has contributed his amoral legal skills to the transfer of Edgar's castle to the Ashtons. His Shylockian answer to Caleb's plea for supplies reveals his determination to make the most of hurly-burly innovation. " The writer stuck to the contents of his feu-charters; he could not see it: 'twas not in the bond." And he reminds Caleb " that new times were not as old times; that they lived on the south of the Forth, and far from the Highlands. . . ." [27]

Dingwall's greed is shared by his fellow-villagers. There is a general hunger for political patronage and a morbid predatory zeal. Just as Dingwall himself looks forward to the death of the

[23] *B.L.*, ch. 11.   [24] *B.L.*, ch. 12.   [25] *B.L.*, ch. 26.
[26] Lockhart, III. 358.   [27] *B.L.*, ch. 12.

county's sheriff-clerk,[28] so Gibbie Girder seeks a sinecure as cooper to the Queen's stores and happily profits from the death of the incumbent.[29]   Even the clergyman Peter Bide-the-Bent is said to have his eye upon " a neighbouring preferment, where the incumbent was sickly." [30]   The greed of the other villagers is equally intense.   Their thirst for political favours leads them to abandon their hostility to Edgar when they hear of his connexion with the Marquis, for they anticipate " a shower of preferment, which hereafter was to leave the rest of Scotland dry, in order to distil its rich dews on the village of Wolf's Hope under Lammermoor." [31]

Such passages are in the vein of realistic social fiction, superbly realised through Scott's fine interiors and pungent lower-class dialogue.   But *The Bride of Lammermoor* is also saturated with the elements of Gothic fiction, and these elements reinforce our sympathy for Edgar as a victim of historical processes and social injustice.   Wolf's Crag, Ravenswood's gloomy fortress by the sea, glimmers in the moonlight " like the sheeted spectre of some huge giant," an emblem of the Ravenswoods and all like them. Caleb calls it " a strength for the Lord of Ravenswood to flee until—that is, no to *flee*, but to retreat until in troublous times, like the present, when it was ill convenient for him to live farther in the country in ony of his better and mair principal manors. . . ." [32]   Here Caleb implies that Edgar has literally been pushed to the edge of the land by his enemies; and when we remember who these enemies are, and how, by legal skulduggery, they have managed to separate him from his other properties, the spectacle of the decayed fortress arouses our sympathy for Edgar as the victim of the new opportunists.

Another Gothic feature of *The Bride* is the character of Blind Alice, an old retainer of the Ravenswoods who stays on the estate even after it has passed into Ashton's hands and who laments the decline of her former masters.   She is a female Tiresias with real prophetic powers, and she makes it clear that her acquaintance with the occult has not dulled her historical

---

[28] *B.L.*, ch. 25.   [29] *B.L.*, chs. 13, 25.   [30] *B.L.*, ch. 26.
[31] *Ibid.*   [32] *B.L.*, ch. 7.

sense or her political virulence. When she overhears that she has been accused of witchcraft, she becomes defiant: " If the usurer, and the oppressor, and the grinder of the poor man's face, and the remover of ancient landmarks, and the subverter of ancient houses, were at the same stake with me, I could say, ' Light the fire, in God's name ! ' " [33]   And when she urges Edgar to avoid the Ashtons, her reasons include those of political opposition : " Can you say as Sir William Ashton says, think as he thinks, vote as he votes, and call your father's murderer your worshipful father-in-law and revered patron ? " [34]   Thus Blind Alice, with her true power as soothsayer, is also a Tory social critic conscious of the demands of party loyalty. Conservatism indeed acquires a peculiar authority when the powers and principalities of the air support it!

When we consider *The Bride of Lammermoor* in the light of the situation so emphatically defined by Blind Alice and sym-bolised in the actions of the Ashtons, the Marquis of A——, and the citizens of Wolf's Hope, we see that nowhere in the Waver-ley Novels is there such a pessimistic emphasis upon social change. *The Bride* is the most heavily opinionated of Scott's works. It does not exhibit the tendency of *Waverley* and *Old Mortality* to find merit on both sides of a political or social conflict. Edgar and Caleb may have been rendered obsolete by the movement of history, their opposites may represent " the wave of the future," but the reader is not encouraged either to rejoice or to remain neutral.

Such singleness of implication is interestingly reinforced by narrowness of range. The world of *The Bride* is provincial ; after the breadth of *The Heart of Midlothian* we seem to be scuttling back to the village environment of *The Antiquary*, although that environment has now lost its air of muddled geniality. We know *The Bride* was composed during a severe illness, but that fact explains little, for *Rob Roy* was also com-posed during a time of illness.[35] Why the intense, isolated gloom, culminating in the first totally convincing conclusion—the death of Ravenswood—that we have so far encountered ?

[33] *B.L.*, ch. 19.   [34] *Ibid.*   [35] Lockhart, III. 201.

H

One answer may suggest itself. Of all the Scottish novels, *The Bride* depicts a period closest to the year 1707, when Scotland became the first sovereign nation in European history to surrender its independence voluntarily. This event did, in a sense, make possible the confusion and venality Jeanie Deans was forced to confront. Scott, who built his boyish fantasies on the images of fleeing Southrons,[36] could hardly have been unaware of the special qualities of that time. We can read in Lockhart of his intense reactions to his first sight of the Scottish regalia,[37] and we may conclude that *The Bride* is really a lamentation over the death of ancient Scottish strength and virtue in a world governed by rich money-snobs with connexions in the corrupt and dominant city of London.

I suspect a deep current of nationalism in *The Bride of Lammermoor*, but it is of a very peculiar kind, and it is qualified by the same impulse to assert the British idea that lies behind Jeanie's journey to the Queen. Thus when the Ashtons obtain legal advantages over the Ravenswoods they can still be shaken by an appeal to the House of Peers. For Edgar such a possibility exists only as a useful threat,[38] but the idea of a British body to which an appeal can be made against the corruptions of local injustice corresponds to the situation in *The Heart of Midlothian* in which a British Queen is given a similar role, and Scott implies full endorsement. Nationalism, after all, is the rallying cry of the fearful *parvenu* Ashton, who protests against the intervention of a " foreign court of appeal."[39]

The truth is that the conservatism of *The Bride of Lammermoor* is too profound to be encompassed by any of the political terms of the eighteenth century or, indeed, of the contemporary world. The Goddess Mutability mocks at such names as " Whig " and " Jacobite " and turns them indifferently upon her wheel. They are, as Edgar in one of his rare forward-looking moments hopes they will become, nicknames for the canting use of coffee-house politicians.[40] We may justifiably interpret Scott's com-

---

[36] *The Poetical Works of Sir Walter Scott*, London 1904, p. 115. See also Lockhart, I. 70.   [37] Lockhart, III. 212-14.

[38] *B.L.*, ch. 16.   [39] *B.L.*, ch. 27.   [40] *B.L.*, ch. 8.

parison of Scotland to an Irish estate as the expression of a desire for a Scottish king on Scottish soil. But such a desire, once articulated, becomes a faction *in ovo*. Scott's discontent is enough to swallow up 1707, 1688, and 1603. He longs for locality, presence, and an assumed authority beyond the reach even of the rhetoric of Burke.

The consequence of such a longing is an irrational and arbitrary development of the royalist implications of *The Heart of Midlothian*. The theory advanced in Chapter 2, that the presence of a king inevitably deters factionalism is questionable by any standards, but we may go farther and note that it is implicitly refuted in *Kenilworth*, *The Fortunes of Nigel*, *Peveril of the Peak*, and *Quentin Durward*, where Elizabeth I, James VI and I, Charles II, and Louis XI of France seem to breed factions wherever they turn. (In his *History of Scotland* Scott even tells of similar divisions flourishing in the court of James *before* he went to London.)[41] We need no more evidence than this that if Scott, as a historical novelist, assumed an obligation to deal justly with the gross and irrefutable facts of history, the atmospheres of his tales and the fates of his heroes were in his own hands and followed the trajectory of his own imagination.

As with his heroes, so with his heroines. Had Scott done his best to create a counter-image to Jeanie Deans, he could have done no better than Lucy, whose passive quietism could fulfil itself only in death. None of Scott's many fictional lyrics suits the mood of its novel more than hers:

> Look not thou on beauty's charming,
> Sit thou still when kings are arming,
> Taste not when the wine-cup glistens,
> Speak not when the people listens,
> Stop thine ear against the singer,
> From the red gold keep thy finger,
> Vacant heart, and hand, and eye,
> Easy live and quiet die.[42]

---

[41] *The History of Scotland*, Philadelphia 1830, Vol. II. *passim*.
[42] *B.L.*, ch. 3.

The Bride of Lammermoor is a climax of reactionary despair. It offers a very dark answer to those preceding works that depict an amiable compromise between past and present, and a reader might legitimately wonder where Scott would turn next. Scott, of course, was too inventive to be trapped in any dead ends, and he was soon to have no trouble carrying his readers with him into his own colourful recreation of the Middle Ages. Nevertheless, it is necessary to know *The Bride* in order to understand the much later *Redgauntlet*, for the Scottish novels form a sequence that follows its own emotional course despite distractions.

Within the Scottish sequence there can be no question of *The Bride's* significance. That part of Scott's mind that hated innovation absolutely—that wept before Jeffrey at the loss of the past [43]—finds expression here. And by releasing the inhibitions that elsewhere might control the expression of that hatred Scott achieved an integrity of style and structure that he had fallen short of since *Waverley*. This achievement is clearest in the conclusion. By all reasonable canons of fiction it is the most convincing Scott was to produce until *Redgauntlet*. It reaches its climax in Ch. 33, when Edgar returns to confront the broken Lucy just as her betrothal to Bucklaw is being formalised. Scott's rhetoric here is distinguished by its controlled operatic rage, and it demands to be accepted on its own terms or not at all :

> " Sir William Ashton," said Ravenswood, " I pray you, and all who hear me, that you will not mistake my purpose. If this young lady, of her own free will, desires the restoration of this contract, as her letter would seem to imply, there is not a withered leaf which this autumn wind strews on the heath that is more valueless in my eyes. But I must and will hear the truth from her own mouth ; without this satisfaction I will not leave this spot. Murder me by numbers you possibly may ; but I am an armed man—I am a desperate man, and I will not die without ample vengeance. This is my resolution, take it

[43] Lockhart, I. 487–8.

as you may. I WILL hear her determination from her own mouth ; from her own mouth, alone, and without witnesses, will I hear it. Now, choose," he said, drawing his sword with the right hand, and, with the left, by the same motion taking a pistol from his belt and cocking it, but turning the point of one weapon and the muzzle of the other to the ground—" choose if you will have this hall floated with blood, or if you will grant me the decisive interview with my affianced bride which the laws of God and the country alike entitle me to demand." [44]

Such sonorous language has its corollary in the sheer solidity of Scott's narrative line. *The Bride* may be compared in this respect with *Old Mortality*, which falls into spasms as it nears its end. If Scott, as Karl Kroeber insists,[45] preferred the direct, forward-moving narrative as the fictional emblem of historical process, then *The Bride* represents the resonant fulfilment of his irrational and anti-modern feelings. In the two stark concluding chapters Lucy dies insane, Edgar rides into the Kelpie's Flow, and the three hags gleefully intone the Fate *motif*. Incidents like these reveal Scott in a realm of his own, far beyond facile categories of acceptance or escapism. They lay bare more clearly than anything else in Scott's work the basic energising dissatisfaction that lies behind the Waverley Novels.

[44] *B.L.*, ch. 33.   [45] See Ch. 4, above, p. 64.

8

A LEGEND OF MONTROSE

"I exceedingly admire Captain Dalgetty."

— Coleridge

The companion novel of *The Bride of Lammermoor* is relatively light in substance. It is also unique in its discordant juxtaposition of widely divergent character types in a remote setting. Scott's original intention, as outlined in his Introduction, was to build a novel around the conflict between Lord Kilpont, Earl of Menteith, and James Stewart of Ardvoirlich, with additional material from the history of the latter. These two noblemen, both of whom served in the Royalist army of the Duke of Montrose, were supposed to be fast friends. But shortly after Montrose's victory at Tippermuir, in 1644, Stewart stabbed his companion to death. His motives for this deed were obscure. Stewart was the son of a woman who had seen her murdered brother's head after it had been placed on her banquet table, with its mouth stuffed full of bread and cheese, by members of the outlawed Clan MacGregor. The MacGregors considered themselves as owing vengeance to every loyal family in their vicinity.

Out of these two themes—the relationship between Kilpont and Stewart and the enmity of the MacEagh family of Clan MacGregor against the Stewarts and their neighbours—Scott

designed his main plot. He solved one problem in the original
material by giving Allan M'Aulay, the character derived from
James Stewart, a motive for attacking Menteith. Scott introduced
a love triangle involving M'Aulay, Menteith, and Annot Lyle,
a beautiful Highland girl of uncertain birth. M'Aulay stabs
Menteith partly because of jealousy. Another difficulty lay in
the lack of any precise connexion between the MacGregors and
Menteith. Scott solved this problem as well as he could by
making Ranald MacEagh and his people the sworn enemies of
the M'Aulays, the Menteiths, the Campbells, and all the other
western clans. The Campbells have, like the M'Aulays, suffered
from their attacks,[1] and Ranald's own plan is to use Annot Lyle
as a means of inducing M'Aulay and Menteith to destroy each
other.[2] Having worked his material into a passably coherent
plot idea, Scott then set it against a background of civil war.
M'Aulay and Menteith serve in Montrose's army during the
winter campaign that culminated in Montrose's victory over
the forces of Campbell and Argyle near Inverlochy Castle in
the Highlands.[3]

But to discuss Scott's plotting devices is to say very little
about the actual structure of *A Legend of Montrose*. It is Dugald
Dalgetty, a man with no ancestral connexions with the above
characters, who dominates the novel. He comes upon the scene
with Menteith and Montrose in Ch. 2, and is present in nearly all
the subsequent chapters. At first he assumes the role of an
obtrusive but essentially secondary humorous character. Although Montrose's first act is his attempt to get Dalgetty to join
the Royalists,[4] the remainder of these chapters is largely devoted
to the preparations of the Royalists for combat, the introduction
of the M'Aulays, and the sketching of Allan's dark and wilful
character,[5] and the introduction of Annot Lyle.[6] Scott is as yet
close to his sources. But in Ch. 8 we learn that someone must
go as envoy to discuss terms of truce with the Marquis of Argyle,
and Dalgetty is chosen. Shortly afterwards[7] he sets out on his

---

[1] *L.M.*, ch. 13. [2] *L.M.*, ch. 17. [3] *L.M.*, ch. 19.
[4] *L.M.*, ch. 3. [5] *L.M.*, chs. 4-5. [6] *L.M.*, ch. 6.
[7] *L.M.*, ch. 10.

mission. From this point he is in full command. Only after the battle does Scott return to the affairs of Menteith, M'Aulay, and Annot Lyle. We are duly informed that Annot is the daughter of Sir Duncan Campbell,[8] and Menteith becomes free to wed her. The moment before the ceremony the jealous Allan stabs the bridegroom.[9] But Scott, having followed the career of the exhilarating Dalgetty, was in no mood for tragedy. We learn that the wound was not fatal, and the work ends happily.

The stabbing of a bridegroom inevitably suggests *The Bride of Lammermoor*. But the parallel is a superficial one. Besides the obvious differences in circumstances there is the character of Allan M'Aulay to be considered. Allan is a gloomy young madman involved in a feud with the MacEagh clan.[10] His gift of prophecy, another apparent link with the *Bride*, leads him to believe that someone, whom he later discovers to be himself, will eventually kill Menteith with his dirk.[11] But Scott, as we have seen, calmly allows the prophecy to go unfulfilled, thus providing a sharp contrast with the previous work. Actually, his concentration upon Dalgetty may have saved the novel. An excerpt from a conversation between Allan and Ranald MacEagh is an example of high rhetoric that lacks the fine inevitability of Ravenswood's address to the Ashtons. Allan has just been told that he is the Highlander who will kill Menteith :

> " But it is impossible ! Were I to read the record in the eternal book of fate, I would declare it impossible : we are bound by the ties of blood, and by a hundred ties more intimate ; we have stood side by side in battle, and our swords have reeked with the blood of the same enemies ; it is IMPOSSIBLE I should harm him ! "
>
> " That you WILL do so," answered Ranald, " is certain, though the cause be hid in the darkness of futurity. ...."[12]

After reading this I consider it fortunate that the novel is so largely governed by the exploits of Dalgetty, and it is a pleasure

[8] *L.M.*, ch. 21.   [9] *L.M.*, ch. 23.   [10] *L.M.*, ch. 5.
[11] *L.M.*, chs. 6, 17.   [12] *L.M.*, ch. 17.

to be able to cite Coleridge for support. He was of the opinion that " if Sir Walter Scott could on any fair ground be compared with Shakespeare, I should select the character of Dalgetty as best supporting the claim. Brave, enterprising, intrepid, brisk to act, stubborn in endurance: these qualities, virtues in a soldier, grounded on wrong principles, but yet *principles*. . . . I exceedingly admire Captain Dalgetty." [13]

Coleridge has rightly emphasized the Captain's military skill and daring. Dalgetty is a complete success in his profession. The novel is largely centred, not only on his personality, but also upon his exploits and triumphs. Besides doing so much to win Montrose's battle for him by his incredible feat of leading a troop of horse through the Highlands in the dead of winter,[14] he outwits the Marquis of Argyle in his own dungeon, escapes with Ranald MacEagh,[15] and gathers military intelligence of the greatest use to Montrose.[16] Scott refrains from pushing his exploits too far. When the Rittmaster finds himself the member of an ambush party of MacEagh's tribe he is free with his advice, contemptuous of their primitive bows and arrows. But his advice is not heeded, he is wounded, and the ambush succeeds without him.[17]

Dalgetty, however, fights for money and plunder. His sense of honour is strict, but entirely commercial; hence he is out of place in a world of intense tribal loyalties. At the end of the novel we are told that Dalgetty would have been executed by the Covenanters had his friends not discovered that his contract with the King would expire in a short time and that he would then be free to join the opposing army of the Kirk. His enlistment in that army immediately followed the expiration of his previous contract. Coleridge understandably admired the effect of such mercenary and legalistic values upon his response to the toasting of King Charles :

" Gentlemen cavaliers," he said, " I drink these healths,

---

[13] *Coleridge's Miscellaneous Criticism*, ed. T. M. Raysor, Cambridge, (Mass.) 1936, p. 328. [14] *L.M.*, ch. 17. [15] *Ibid.*
[16] *L.M.*, chs. 14. 16. [17] *L.M.*, ch. 14.

primo, both out of respect to this honourable and
hospitable roof-tree, and, *secundo*, because I hold it not
good to be preceese in such matters, *inter pocula*; but I
protest, agreeable to the warrandice granted by this
honourable lord, that it will be free to me, notwithstanding my present complaisance, to take service with
the Covenanters to-morrow, providing I shall be so
minded.[18]

Dalgetty is also an unsettled figure who, without being
consciously lonely, is always betraying his loneliness.   His
survey of his past military career in Ch. 2 reveals an acquaintance
with European society that is broader, though not deeper, than
any figure we have encountered in the Waverley Novels so far.
The virtues of provincialism are not his.   The inevitable result
of such an uncentred existence is that his only intimate friend is
the beast on which he rides.   It is well that Gustavus, his horse,
is capable of " the discretion of a Christian,"[19] for Dalgetty is
dependent upon him for more than transportation.   Refusing to
let ordinary grooms or stable-keepers attend to him, Dalgetty
observes that " we are old friends and fellow-travellers, and, as
I often need the use of his legs, I always lend him in my turn the
service of my tongue to call for whatever he has occasion for.
. . ."[20]   When, as he and Ranald are about to enter the Highland
area, it becomes necessary to leave Gustavus to the care of others,
Dalgetty actually experiences a wave of sentiment:

> " Give your horse to the gillie," said Ranald MacEagh;
> " your life depends upon it."
>   " Och ! och ! " exclaimed the despairing veteran.
> " Eheu ! as we are used to say at Marischal College, must
> I leave Gustavus in such grooming ? "
>   " Are you frantic, to lose time thus ? " said his guide.
> " Do we stand on friend's ground, that you should part
> with your horse as if he were your brother ?   I tell you,
> you shall have him again; but if you never saw the animal,

[18] *L.M.*, ch. 5; *Coleridge's Miscellaneous Criticism*, ed. Raysor, p. 328.
[19] *L.M.*, ch. 11.   [20] *L.M.*, ch. 4.

is not life better than the best colt ever mare foaled ? "

"And that is true too, mine honest friend," sighed Dalgetty ; "yet if you knew but the value of Gustavus, and the things we two have done and suffered together. See, he turns back to look at me ! Be kind to him, my good breechless friend, and I will requite you well." So saying, and withal sniffling a little to swallow his grief, he turned from the heartrending spectacle to follow his guide.[21]

But once again Scott avoids pushing Dalgetty too far. When Gustavus is killed at Inverlochy he prepares to pay him a last visit :

> "Not with the purpose of going through the cere-
> monial of interment ? " said the Marquis, who did not
> know how far Sir Dugald's enthusiasm might lead him.
> "Consider, our brave fellows themselves will have but a
> hasty burial."
> "Your Excellency will pardon me," said Dalgetty ;
> "my purpose is less romantic. I go to divide poor
> Gustavus's legacy with the fowls of heaven, leaving the
> flesh to them and reserving to myself his hide ; which, in
> token of affectionate remembrance, I purpose to form
> into a cassock and trowsers, after the Tartar fashion, to
> be worn under my armour, in respect my nether garments
> are at present shamefully the worse of the wear." [22]

Such a man has little in common, besides soldiering, with Montrose and Menteith. But with Ranald MacEagh and his tribe Dalgetty seems even more out of tune. On the subject of military tactics there is no agreement, for Dalgetty scorns the clan's " irregular Scythian fashion of warfare," [23] until he sees its effectiveness in the Highland skirmish. Nor can Dalgetty under- stand in the least the Highlander's deep pagan devotion to his hills and forests. He is totally uninterested in the beauties of

<hr />

[21] *L.M.*, ch. 14. [22] *L.M.*, ch. 20. [23] *L.M.*, ch. 13.

Loch Fine,[24] and is repulsed by Ranald's religious feeling for the mountain mist:

> "... Ranald MacEagh is my name—that is, Ranald
> Son of the Mist."
>   " Son of the Mist ! " ejaculated Dalgetty. " Son of
> utter darkness, say I." [25]

And there is a strange and haunting contrast between different sensibilities in an episode near the end of the novel, when Ranald is about to die. Dugald has protested against Ranald's exhortation to his grandson to pursue their clan's enemies with vengeance:

> The only answer of the dying man . . . was a request
> to be raised to such a position that he might obtain a
> view from the window of the castle. The deep frost
> mist, which had long settled upon the tops of the moun-
> tains, was now rolling down each rugged glen and
> gully, where the craggy ridges showed their black and
> irregular outline, like desert islands rising above the
> ocean of vapour. " Spirit of the Mist ! " said Ranald
> MacEagh, " called by our race our father and our
> preserver, receive into thy tabernacle of clouds, when
> this pang is over, him whom in life thou has so often
> sheltered." So saying, he sunk back into the arms of
> those who upheld him, spoke no further word, but turned
> his face to the wall for a short space.
>   " I believe," said Dalgetty, " my friend Ranald will
> be found in his heart to be little better than a heathen."
> And he renewed his proposal to procure him the assist-
> ance of Dr Wisheart, Montrose's military chaplain;
> " a man," said Sir Dugald, " very clever in his exercise,
> and who will do execution on your sins in less time
> than I could smoke a pipe of tobacco." [26]

Such an exchange would seem to be another manifestation of Scott's delight in contradictions. On the one hand, a clansman

[24] *L.M.*, ch. 11.   [25] *L.M.*, ch. 13.   [26] *L.M.*, ch. 22.

possessing a deep bond of unity with his clan and his locality ; on the other a rootless mercenary with a little Latin. However, it is significant that Dalgetty *has* run away with the story—and I intend a larger reference than to Scott's permissiveness in allowing his humours full play. Dalgetty poses a crucial question to the values of his supposed moral superiors, with their infantile fanaticisms of creed, party, or clan. Even his pedantry (he is an alumnus of Marischal College) is relevant to his role. Mr Francis Hart finds this characteristic a bore.[27] I do not. It is a refreshing intrusion into a world of quarrelling provincials of a larger European view of things, distorted though it may be. He knows something of military and contractual codes, of Renaissance military tactics, of scholastic reasoning, and he clearly loves an international language. Even his commercial motives, in the absence of any vitally realised value system, seem cosmopolitan and enlightened. It is not surprising that Scott, composing *Montrose* in physical pain, found Dalgetty a relief. It is only to be regretted that as author he seems to endorse for a moment the utterly contemptible contempt that Menteith expresses for the man who had saved his cause.[28] Fortunately, however, it is Dalgetty who has the novel's last word, risking martyrdom over the terms of his enlistment, and eventually living to garrulous old age " very full of interminable stories about the immortal Gustavus Adolphus, the Lion of the North, and the Bulwark of the Protestant Faith."

Scott's delight in Dalgetty is in part a rebellion against fanaticism and in part an escape from the tragic implications of *The Bride*. In both Dalgetty and his insistence on a happy ending, Scott shows resilience, and a desire to escape the muddy problems of his Scottish material. Considering *The Bride* and *Montrose* together we can understand why his next work took him out of Scotland entirely.

[27] F. R. Hart, *Scott's Novels : The Plotting of Historical Survival*, Charlottesville 1966, p. 125.

[28] *L.M.*, ch. 20.

9

TWO NON-SCOTTISH
NOVELS

" I wonder who wrote Quentin Durward ? "

— Mark Twain

When Francis Jeffrey, reviewing *Ivanhoe*, complained of its
" vulgar staple of armed knights, and jolly friars or woodsmen,
imprisoned damsels, lawless barons, collared serfs, and house-
hold fools," he anticipated an attitude towards non-Scottish
Waverley Novels that was to prevail for generations.[1] It is all
the more refreshing, therefore, that Mr Hart has recently challenged the assumption that Scott is lost away from Scotland and
that his medievalism is mere " Tushery." [2] Even a just view of
things can be spoiled by complacent repetition.

Nevertheless, I see no reason yet to do more than modify
orthodox opinion. Even though *The Black Dwarf* and *St Ronan's
Well* seem poor things beside *Quentin Durward*, it is in seven-
teenth- and eighteenth-century Scotland that Scott finds matter

---

[1] See Francis Jeffrey, *Contributions to the Edinburgh Review.* 4 vols.
London 1844, III. 474 ; and James T. Hillhouse, *The Waverley Novels and
their Critics*, Minneapolis 1936, p. 47.

[2] F. R. Hart, " *The Fair Maid*, Manzoni's *Betrothed*, and the Grounds
of Waverley Criticism ", in *Nineteenth-Century Fiction*, XVIII (1963). p. 106 ;
see also F. R. Hart, *Scott's Novels* pp. 150-1.

of the most significant complexity, simply because Scotland itself performs a dramatic role in all events. (Hence, perhaps, the real importance to Scott of Maria Edgeworth ; the substitution of genuine Irishmen for theatrical *clichés* meant that Ireland itself became a fictional " character.")

Moreover, Francis R. Hart has chosen *The Fair Maid of Perth* to illustrate the riches of Scott's exotic novels. It is a shrewd choice—a novel of psychological interest in its presentation of Conachar's understandable revulsion at the deadly, mechanistic horror of a battle to the death between clansmen. In addition, it has some of the Scottish poetry still, as the words of Hector Quhele demonstrate: "See, here is the stick I had from you when we nutted together in the sunny braes of Lednoch, when autumn was young in the year that is gone." [3] And the sustained employment of hand imagery that Hart discovers is indeed an indication of Scott's technical capacities and must be thought of by those who would underrate those capacities.[4] I think, however, that there is a fallacy in assuming that novels can be made more interesting by the diligent searching out of recurrent symbolic *motifs*. All the hand imagery in a shelf of novels will not substitute adequately for the free, opportunistic poetry of Scott's Jenny Dennisons and Edie Ochiltrees. Finally, to say no more for the present, there is one sadly conspicuous void in the medieval and exotic works that can only be acknowledged and regretted : there are, alas, very few Scottish Presbyterians.

I do not intend, however, to justify my preference for the Scottish novels by attacking the others. Leslie Stephen's disapproving reference to the " lavish display of mediaeval upholstery," [5] is invalid, partly because they offer more than that, and partly because I know not a single convincing argument to prove that novelists lack the right to crowd their scenes

[3] *F.M.P.*, ch. 14.

[4] F. R. Hart, " *The Fair Maid...*", pp. 112-14, and *Scott's Novels*, pp. 241-4.

[5] Leslie Stephen, *Hours in a Library*, 3 vols., London and New York 1894, I. 155.

with non-emblematic furniture of all sorts.   G. K. Chesterton
especially praised Scott's love of things in themselves.[6]   This
love is both Homeric and Balzacian.

It is unfortunate, however, that Scott's first medieval work
was *Ivanhoe*—a novel of gusto and confusion.   Ostensibly a tale
of Saxon and Norman, it manages to parade before the reader
most of the stereotypes of " Merrie England "—Richard, Friar
Tuck, Robin Hood, the simple villain Prince John—while also
supposedly revealing the plight of the Jews.   There is matter
enough in the realm of cultural conflict and one critic has seen
Ivanhoe as an anti-medieval work,[7] but in the final analysis it is
sheer John Bullism that carries the day.   Cedric the Saxon, whom
Lady Louisa Stuart called " that worthy forefather of the genuine
English country-gentleman," [8] is proof that Scott could quite
easily and sincerely out-Saxon the Saxons :

> " Good Father Aymer . . . be it known to you, I care
> not for those over-sea refinements, without which I can
> well enough take my pleasure in the woods.   I can wind
> my horn, though I call not the blast either a *recheat* or a
> *mort* ; I can cheer my dogs on the prey, and I can flay and
> quarter the animal when it is brought down, without
> using the newfangled jargon of *curée, arbor, nombles*, and
> all the babble of the fabulous Sir Tristrem." [9]

Scott, a John Bull in his own way, was perfectly happy to
write this, but the effect of triteness and chauvinistic *cliché* is
inescapable, and when to this flaw is added the ambiguity of the
portrayal of Isaac,[10] structural defects such as the failure to
develop the theme of Ivanhoe's disinheritance, and the sheer
vulgarity of the resurrection of Athelstane, *Ivanhoe*, for all its
narrative vigour and its enthronement in school reading lists,

---

[6] G. K. Chesterton, *Varied Types*, London 1903, pp. 167-8.

[7] J. E. Duncan, " The Anti-Romantic in *Ivanhoe* " in *Nineteenth-Century Fiction*, IX (1955), pp. 293-300.   Even Hart, who endorses Duncan's view, finds evidence of uncertainty and confusion in *Ivanhoe*: see *Scott's Novels*, pp. 164-6.   [8] *Letters*, VI. 116 n.   [9] *I.*, ch. 5.

[10] E. Rosenberg, *From Shylock to Svengali : Jewish Stereotypes in English Fiction*, Stanford 1960, pp. 73-102.

seems a confusing commencement of a series of new narrative adventures.

Quentin Durward, on the other hand, reveals that Scott could write of medieval Europe with distinction and authority. The novel represents a brilliant recovery after the comparative failure of *Peveril of the Peak*.[11] Scott gloated over finding " an admirable little corner of history . . . where the vulgar dogs of imitators have no sense to follow me." [12] The corner was the France of Louis XI.

Quentin Durward is the story of a young and destitute Scot who, seeking a master to serve, enrols in Louis's Scots Guard and soon finds himself in the midst of a conflict between the monarch and Charles of Burgundy. Unlike Ivanhoe, Quentin is not wounded and abandoned almost as soon as the principal plot gets under way. In fact he appears in all but six of the thirty-seven chapters, and despite Scott's statement in the Introduction that " the little love intrigue of Quentin is only employed as a means of bringing out the story," he represents a strong element of continuity.

If the hero is not lost sight of, neither is the central theme, that of the conflict between Louis and Charles—policy and wit against strength and choler. This conflict comes vigorously into the open in chapter eight when Crèvecœur throws down the gauntlet of his master to Louis, and is not out of our minds until the final chapter. Furthermore, the nature of the opposition between Louis and Charles is not rendered impure by irrelevant associations. Being away from Britain, Scott is less tempted into opportunistic appeals to British nationalism. Charles is a blunt man, but he is no " worthy forefather of the genuine English country-gentleman," and Louis is a crafty ruler, but not a degraded symbol of the French national character to Charles, Scott, or the reader.

In *Quentin Durward*, as in *Ivanhoe*, there is much action and bloodshed, centred particularly in the rising at Liège which, broadly speaking, occupies Chs. 19 to 22, and the storming of that city by the forces of Louis and Charles, which is described,

11 Lockhart, IV. 85-6, 117-18.   12 *Letters*, vii. 308.

I

with interludes, in the last two chapters. Both battles arise out
of the interests and passions of individuals and groups important
to the story, and the significance of the rebellion of the Liègeois
and the murder of the Bishop weighs heavily upon the relations
between Louis and Charles at the interview in Péronne. And
unlike *Ivanhoe*, in which the action constantly accelerates and
slackens before and after such events as the tournament at Ashby,
the siege of Torquilstone, the trial of Rebecca, and the final (and
ineffectual) combat between hero and villain, *Quentin Durward*
restricts itself to two scenes of battle, both organically related
to the main plot. The final battle of Liège comes as a release from
the quieter tensions of the council chamber, and for all the
bloodiness of the battle *ensembles* in the closing pages, the effect
is that of a clearing of the air.

Besides these structural advantages, *Quentin Durward* has
some characters of great validity. Louis XI, drawn in part after
Phillipe de Comines, is not a king lost in the mists of legend.
Actually Scott, whatever he may feel about the moral stature of
Louis, makes him the hero of his tale in a way that Quentin is
not. Louis is a bold ruler somewhat ahead of his time. He is
among those " who were the first to ridicule and abandon the
self-denying principles in which the young knight was instructed."
In other words, he was one of the first who rejected the chivalric
ideal and its moral implications. Hence he relies on the strength
of his mind rather than on that of his arm, and since Scott con-
tinually places him in embarrassing and dangerous positions,
even violating historical chronology so that Charles can learn
of the murder of his Bishop while Louis is in his power,[13] the
reader is bound to regard him with some of the sympathy due to
a David going against Goliath. Perhaps we begin to take this
attitude during the encounter between Louis and the high-
handed Crèvecœur, when the latter delivers Charles's defiance.
The whole tone of the envoy's address to Louis reveals that
Charles is spoiling for a row and thinks to have one by means of
an insulting disavowal of all allegiance to the French King :

[13] Scott confesses his violation in *Q.D.*, Appendix, Note 31.

" I, Philip Crèvecœur of Cordès, Count of the Empire,
and Knight of the honourable and princely Order of the
Golden Fleece, in the name of the most puissant Lord
and Prince, Charles, [here follows a resounding series of
titles] do give you, Louis, King of France, openly to
know, that, you having refused to remedy the various griefs,
wrongs, and offences done and wrought by you, or by
and through your aid, suggestion, and instigation, against
the said Duke and his loving subjects, he, by my mouth,
renounces all allegiance and fealty towards your crown
and dignity, pronounces you false and faithless, and
defies you as a prince and as a man. There lies my gage,
in evidence of what I have said." [14]

While the court is in tumult Crèvecœur delivers a parting insult
and leaves. Louis, however, refuses to allow any of his knights
to lift the gauntlet, insisting it be returned by Cardinal Balue,
and while Dunois and Crawford are still in a passion he is already
thinking of persuading so gallant a soldier as Crèvecœur into
his own service. Then he signals for a hunt to begin, thus
providing an outlet for pent-up emotions. The same qualities
of coolness and intelligence are revealed to an even greater extent
in the scene at Péronne, when Charles learns of the Bishop's
murder; and the fact that Louis and his few companions are
completely at the mercy of Charles, and that his chivalric de-
fenders, led by Dunois and Crawford, are ready to begin a hope-
less and ruinous struggle then and there, gives Louis the stature
of a heroic underdog as he wins time for himself.[15]

It is sometimes confusing to read Scott's introductions. He
wrote that of *Quentin Durward* when he was near the end of his
life, ill and weary, and he seems to regard Louis almost as a
personal enemy. "That sovereign," he writes, "was of a
character so purely selfish—so guiltless of entertaining any
purpose unconnected with his ambition, covetousness, and desire
of selfish enjoyment, that he almost seems an incarnation of the
devil himself, permitted to do his utmost to corrupt our ideas of

[14] *Q.D.*, ch. 8. [15] *Q.D.*, ch. 27.

honour in its very source." And Scott goes on to suggest that
he may be a blacker example of evil than Milton's Satan, who
possesses "something which elevates and dignifies his wickedness." He who reads the novel after this may easily feel that
Scott is committing the error many of his Romantic contemporaries attributed to Milton, that of making his villain his hero.
He does, however, portray Louis's Machiavellianism in the
strongest possible colours in that interview with Oliver le Dain
in which he plots the marriage of Isabelle to William de la Marck,[16]
although Louis has so much policy on his mind that he has much
less time to indulge in the conventional histrionics of villainy
than had Prince John of *Ivanhoe*. Moreover, after the explosion
at Péronne when Charles learns of events at Liège, Louis's
behaviour is utterly reprehensible. He has calmed the storm
caused by Charles's wrath and the noble defiance of Dunois and
Crawford, and Scott (in the spirit of Burke instructing the French
in their own virtues) [17] has carefully pointed out the difference
between the behaviour of the knights, who serve Louis faith-
fully on the principles of chivalry, and that of Oliver le Dain,
Tristan l'Hermite, Trois-Eschelles, Petit-André, and Galeotti,
who have been noticeably silent and watchful. Louis, about to
be imprisoned, is told that he is allowed six attendants.

> "Then," said the King, looking around him, and
> thinking for a moment, "I desire the attendance of Oliver
> le Dain, of a private of my Life Guard, called Balafré,
> who may be unarmed if you will, of Tristan l'Hermite,
> with two of his people, and my right loyal and trusty
> philosopher, Martius Galeotti." [18]

Upon which the jester Le Glorieux makes a comment to Crèvecœur which is appropriate enough :

> "A panderly barber, a Scottish hired cut-throat, a chief
> hangman and his two assistants, and a thieving charlatan.

---

[16] *Q.D.*, ch. 12.
[17] E. Burke, *Reflections on the Revolution in France*, New York (Liberal
Arts Press) 1955, p. 41.   [18] *Q.D.*, ch. 27.

I will along with you, Crèvecœur, and take a lesson in the degrees of roguery, from observing your skill in marshalling them. The devil himself could scarce have summoned such a synod, or have been a better president amongst them." [19]

And this scene is soon followed by the attempts of Louis to do away with Galeotti. It would appear that Scott, aware that his readers (as well as the author!) may have been forgetting the nature of the serpent in admiration for his cunning, was doing his best to sharpen our sense of his wickedness. It won't do, however. Louis, despite the exaggerated nature of many of his acts—the assumption of disguise in the early chapters, the excessively Machiavellian flavour of many of his utterances, and the juvenile mumming of the attempt to murder Galeotti—stands forth as an appealing scoundrel, and we are happy to see him have his way in the end.

The greatest danger to Louis lies in the unruly tempers of Charles of Burgundy and William de la Marck. The former is a conventional angry man, whose speech breaks into rant under provocation, as in his answer to Louis after the news of the Bishop's death has been brought to Péronne :

" These news, fair cousin, have staggered your reason."
" No ! " replied the Duke, in a terrible tone, " but they have awakened a just resentment, which I have too long suffered to be stifled by trivial considerations of circumstance and place. Murderer of thy brother !—rebel against thy parent !—tyrant over thy subjects !—treacherous ally !—perjured king !— dishonoured gentlemen !—thou art in my power, and I thank God for it." [20]

As for De la Marck, the Wild Boar of Ardennes, Scott does his best to make him appear worthy of his popular title :

" Hast thou yet done ? " said De la Marck, fiercely interrupting him, and stamping with his foot.
" No," answered the prelate, " for I have not yet told

[19] *Ibid.*   [20] *Ibid.*

thee the terms which you demanded to hear from me."

"Go on," said De la Marck; "and let the terms please
me better than the preface, or woe to thy grey head!"
And flinging himself back in his seat, he grinded his
teeth till the foam flew from his lips, as from the tusks
of the savage animal whose name and spoils he wore.[21]

The atmosphere of high melodrama that pervades this scene in
which the axe falls upon the poor Bishop is somewhat enhanced
by the fact that the Wild Boar begins matters by hanging a
luckless offender to the stanchions of a large window in the hall.
"His body still hung there when Quentin and the others entered
the hall, and intercepting the pale moonbeam, threw on the
castle-floor an uncertain shadow, which dubiously, yet fearfully,
intimated the nature of the substance that produced it." Yet De
la Marck has a genuinely impressive moment just before his death
in the final battle at Liège:

> It was just when De la Marck, retiring through this
> infernal scene, had passed the door of a small chapel of
> peculiar sanctity, that the shouts of "France—France!
> Burgundy—Burgundy!" apprized him that his retreat
> was cut off. "Conrad," he said, "take all the men with
> you. Charge yonder fellows roundly, and break through
> if you can; with me it is over. I am man enough, now
> that I am brought to bay, to send some of these vagabond
> Scots to hell before me." [22]

In part De la Marck's speech illustrates the truth of Ruskin's
remark that Scott enjoys rebellion as long as it isn't done "on
principle and in form." [23]   De la Marck would thus deserve his
closing lines on semi-political grounds. But De la Marck here
is also like Macbeth, asserting his achieved identity in a waste-
land of death and defeat. It is Scott who had the generosity to
allow the Wild Boar this moment of dignity, and the humanity
of the gesture is typical.

[21] *Q.D.*, ch. 22.   [22] *Q.D.*, ch. 37.
[23] J. Ruskin, *Works*, v. 345.

Thrust into this world in which policy wars with brutality is a hero of the Edward Waverley type who must experience the ridicule of his fondest dreams by older and wiser Count Crève-cœur.[24] In one respect, however, Quentin, despite his warrior's profession, reveals the influence of the quietism that we have observed embodied in other novels. Throughout his exchanges with his uncle Le Balafré we are reminded that Quentin was brought up in a monastery, where he received instruction in letters and ethics that set him apart from most of his contemporaries.[25] The degree of emphasis Scott gives this fact indicates that he intends more than a mere circumstantial explanation of Quentin's possibly anachronistic enlightenment. In one passage Scott suggests an interesting connexion between humane feeling and physical debility that reminds us that his own boyhood illness, not to mention later difficulties, may have contributed both to his fascination with violent men and his sense of their futility:

> The lessons of the worthy old monk, better attended to, perhaps, during a long illness and adversity than they might have been in health and success, had given young Durward still farther insight into the duties of humanity towards others. . . .[26]

In describing elsewhere his own early years Scott reveals the advantages of illness as a stimulant to the imagination. As a result of his physical ailments his sensibilities were nourished by travel and by extended intervals of idleness among his good-natured female relatives. His return to Edinburgh after such nourishment was a hard experience demanding strong self-discipline. Still, his mother was there to keep the old memories alive, and they were memories of indolence and creative passivity.[27] Their influence was never to desert him. Lucy Ashton is the still point of a turning world, and even Quentin, the hero of one of Scott's bloodiest novels, has profited from the lessons of a recluse.

---

[24] *Q.D.*, ch. 24.   [25] *Q.D.*, ch. 5.   [26] *Q.D.*, ch. 6.
[27] Lockhart, I. 12-21 *passim.*

When Quentin enrols in Louis's Scottish guard, he finds himself in a congenial group of his own countrymen, and this is a definite advantage to the story. In *Ivanhoe*, Scott had put his country behind him, but here he is able to make sport with his exiles and the reputation they have on the Continent, particularly in the early chapters in which the disguised Louis encounters Durward for the first time. Among the hero's companions the two most prominent are his uncle Ludovic Lesly, called Le Balafré, and the venerable Lord Crawford. The former is in many ways the most successful character in the novel. Being a mercenary soldier without any high reputation for honesty, he reminds us of Captain Dalgetty in *A Legend of Montrose*. Lord Crawford is a more conventional version of the aged and faithful soldier. It is notable that he is given what few scraps of vernacular Scots there are, although an example will show that the full idiom is not exploited :

> " How often . . . will you bring me such ill-winded
> pirns to ravel out ? . . . However, if you must have a
> bargain, I would rather it were with that loon of a
> provost than any one else ; and I blame you less for this
> onslaught than for other frays that you have made,
> Ludovic, for it was but natural and kindlike to help your
> young kinsman. This simple bairn must come to no
> skaith neither ; so give me the roll of the company
> yonder down from the shelf, and we will even add his
> name to the troop, that he may enjoy the privileges." [28]

One cannot help feeling that Scott enjoyed introducing his countrymen into France, just as he enjoyed marching Jeanie Deans into England. One reason for not underrating the " non-Scottish " works as a whole is simply that so often, as De la Marck sadly discovered, they swarm with Scotsmen.

What applies to *Quentin Durward* applies even more decidedly to *The Fortunes of Nigel*. Here the Scots, if the comments of the surlier English characters are to be believed, have invaded England behind James VI and I, and some of the issues raised in

[28] *Q.D.*, ch. 7.

The Heart of Midlothian are seen again in Jacobean London. Significantly, the first chapter tells of a small-scale uprising by the London apprentices against Richie Moniplies, the hero's Scottish servant.

It seems inevitable that Scott, sooner or later, should have written *Nigel*. His Introduction makes clear his sensitivity to the elements of social and intellectual transition in the period. Moreover, his almost encyclopaedic acquaintance with the literature of the period, particularly the drama, gave him a careless idiomatic skill in the handling of speech that approaches his fluency in Lowland Scots. Finally, the man who enjoyed mad pedants, ineffectual antiquaries, and superstitious dominies could hardly have been expected to resist James I, who embodied so many of the same qualities in his royal person.

Nigel first appeared with an " Introductory Epistle " that has its own claim to fame as an intensive discussion of the author's literary faults and virtues by the author himself. The style of the encounter between " Captain Clutterbuck " and the "Author of *Waverley* " is charming, relaxed and contradictory. Here he confesses his awareness that the novel has not lived up to Fielding's hopes for it, his acceptance of his role as public entertainer, and his rebellion against that role in his insistence on the power of his own unconditioned creative impulses.

Nevertheless, there is something deceptive about this Epistle, particularly if it is remembered during the novel that follows. Captain Clutterbuck, for example, mentions *Tom Jones* as a novel in which an effective plan is effectively carried through. The Author replies :

> True, and perhaps *Amelia* also. Fielding had high notions of the dignity of an art which he may be considered as having founded. He challenges a comparison between the novel and the epic. Smollett, Le Sage [Scott has forgotten his dates], and others, emancipating themselves from the strictness of the rules he has laid down, have written rather a history of the miscellaneous adventures which befall an individual in the course of

life. . . . These great masters have been satisfied if they amused the reader upon the road ; though the conclusion only arrived because the tale must have an end. . . .[29]

" The Author " then goes on to align himself with these less disciplined masters, and he later confesses that " there is a demon who seats himself on the feather of my pen when I begin to write, and leads it astray from the purpose." [30]

Now there is an element of truth in this admission, as Dalgetty, whom Scott cites to prove his point, serves to demonstrate. But the plot of *Nigel* itself encourages a curious suspicion of " the Author's " candour. To be sure, there are signs of a forsaken plan in the disappearance of George Heriot as an important agent in the story after his strong emergence as Nigel's present and future benefactor. (In Ch. 13 he is called away to France upon some obscure " business of great importance in the way of his profession " and doesn't return until Ch. 29.) Nevertheless, *Nigel* has one of the most complicated plots Scott ever devised, it is handled with few offences against narrative logic, and, above all, more than any of the Waverley Novels it bears the closest resemblance to *Tom Jones* ! It is Scott's most eloquent tribute to Fielding's narrative method.

In *Tom Jones* Fielding brought a disinherited hero to London, involved him in difficulties that seemed insuperable, and finally rescued him and restored him to his name and lands. Scott, although his Somerset, *i.e.*, Scotland, is not the scene of major events, does exactly the same thing. At the beginning of Fielding's Book 18, Jones is almost universally condemned as a thief, a murderer, and a sexual adventurer. Then Fielding marshals his revelations and saves the situation in approximately sixty pages. Nigel is an impoverished Scot who comes to London to petition King James for the payment of an old debt, the satisfaction of which will enable him to retrieve his mortgaged Scottish estate. The essence of Nigel's trouble lies in the enmity of Lord Dalgarno, who is motivated by considerations of greed that resemble Blifil's. The course of the story can best be

[29] " Introductory Epistle " to *F.N.*   [30] *Ibid.*

understood if we examine Nigel's situation in Ch. 29. He has been imprisoned in the Tower under the following circumstances :

1. He is unable to retrieve his estate as the deadline for the payment of his mortgage approaches.
2. He is universally condemned for having apparently victimised and ruined a London tradesman by means of petty and overcautious gambling.
3. He is held for duelling in the King's park; the established punishment for this crime is the loss of the right hand.
4. The unmarried daughter of an old friend is discovered in his cell disguised as a boy.
5. He is suspected of having seduced a ship chandler's wife.
6. He is suspected of being in some way responsible for the mysterious disappearance of a spinster with 50,000 pounds.
7. He is accused of attempting to kill the King.

Scott allows himself eight chapters to carry Nigel over this Chinese Wall, and, with the help of the mysterious (hence potentially useful) Lady Hermione, he manages his desperate chores fairly well. But how this sort of plotting is to be reconciled with Scott's introductory representation of the "Author of *Waverley*" as one who pipes but as the linnets sing is a mystery in itself. It is enough to point out that anyone who regards Scott as all of a piece in his methods of composing is in the possession of a fine, easily documented, half-truth.

In its historical implications *Nigel* shares some of the complexity that, despite certain introductory flourishes, is for the most part absent from *Quentin Durward*. In his 1831 Introduction Scott refers to a favourite passage by Lady Mary Wortley Montague :

> . . . the most romantic region of every country is that where the mountains unite themselves with the plains or lowlands. For similar reasons, it may be in like manner said that the most picturesque period of history is that when the ancient rough and wild manners of a barbarous age are just becoming innovated upon and contrasted by

the illumination of increased or revived learning and the
instructions of renewed or reformed religion. The strong
contrast produced by the opposition of ancient manners
to those which are gradually subduing them affords the
lights and shadows necessary to give effect to a fictitious
narrative. . . .[31]

He goes on to point out how " Some beams of chivalry . . .
continued to animate and gild the horizon " in the time of
James, but that " while men were taking each other's lives on . . .
punctilios of honour, the hour was already arrived when Bacon
was about to teach the world that they were no longer to reason
from authority to fact, but to establish truth by advancing from
fact to fact, till they fixed an indisputable authority, not from
hypothesis, but from experiment." [32]

This is the historical situation that prevails when Nigel comes
to London to petition for his debt, and Scott, by giving many of
his characters a particular posture with regard to this situation,
and by seeing to it that the situation itself is not forgotten,
constantly reminds the reader of the moral and intellectual issues
which are involved. George Heriot, for example, represents the
new era of trade and commerce at a time when the traditional
manners and beliefs of English feudalism are on their way out.
The importance of this rising world is indicated by the importance of Heriot himself, upon whom James depends so much for
the maintenance of the royal credit, and with whom he adopts
so familiar a manner. Heriot is of the same world as the city
businessmen of *Rob Roy*—willing and able to rescue an ancestral
estate or, if necessary, an entire kingdom. Not only does he do
his best to persuade James to pay his debt to Nigel, but he
constantly reveals a respect for the manners of the feudal past, as
well as a real sense of its virtues. Thus, despite his superiority
to Nigel in age, poise, wealth, and influence, Heriot forgets
neither the deference owed to Nigel because of his blood, nor
the duties imposed upon Nigel by his own high birth. At one
point, when Heriot visits Nigel in the Tower, he angrily upbraids

[31] Introduction (1831) to *F.N.*   [32] *Ibid.*

him for violating the honour of his ancestors.[33] He is also conscious of the way certain other members of the aristocracy live up to their duties. Speaking of Lord Huntinglen and his son Dalgarno, Heriot makes use of a typical Scott image :

> " There live," he said, " the old fashion and the new.
> The father is like a noble old broadsword, but harmed
> with rust, from neglect and inactivity ; the son is your
> modern rapier, well-mounted, fairly gilt, and fashioned
> to the taste of the time—and it is time must evince if the
> metal be as good as the show. God grant it prove so,
> says an old friend to the family." [34]

Such passages as this sound the note of mutability as clearly as anything in Scott. Richie Moniplies, Dalgarno, Lord Hunting-len, and King James demonstrate different attitudes towards the struggle between past and present, and the relations of each to his fellows is affected by his position along the line of progress or decay, as the case may be. Nigel, Dalgarno, and Huntinglen are three representatives of the old feudal aristocracy of Scotland, and each symbolises a particular response to the phenomenon of that system's decline. The inexperienced Nigel invades London and its manifold temptations without ever having had his in-herited ideas challenged. Dalgarno, who has forsaken the ways of his forefathers and is now beyond redemption, is Nigel's tempter. Observe the way in which he ridicules Nigel's desire to return to Scotland after obtaining the money for his estate :

> " You are jesting with me. . . . All the court rings—it
> is needless to mince it—with the extraordinary success of
> your suit, against the highest interest, it is said, now
> influencing the horizon at Whitehall. Men think of you
> —talk of you—fix their eyes on you—ask each other,
> ' Who is this young Scottish lord, who has stepped so
> far in a single day ? ' They augur . . . how high and how
> far you may push your fortune ; and all that you design
> to make of it is to return to Scotland, eat raw oatmeal

[33] *F.N.*, ch. 29.   [34] *F.N.*, ch. 10.

cakes, baked upon a peat-fire, have your hand shaken by
every loon of a blue-bonnet who chooses to dub you
cousin, though your relationship comes by Noah, drink
Scots twopenny ale, eat half-starved red-deer venison,
when you can kill it, ride upon a galloway, and be called
' my right honourable and maist worthy lord ! ' " 35

Dalgarno's position as a spokesman for new fashions at their
worst is not altered by his desire to obtain Nigel's estate for
himself. It is exactly in his attitude towards ancestral lands that
he differs most sharply from his father, Lord Huntinglen, who
expresses himself as follows :

> ". . . my grey beard falls on a cambric ruff and a silken
> doublet, my father's descended upon a buff coat and a
> breastplate. I would not that those days of battle returned ;
> but I should love well to make the oaks of my old forest
> of Dalgarno ring once more with halloo, and horn, and
> hound, and to have the old stone-arched hall return the
> hearty shout of my vassals and tenants, as the bicker and
> the quaigh walked their rounds amongst them." 36

Dalgarno has gone far beyond this. Unlike his father, he has
ruptured his connexion with the old Scotland so completely that
he can view his home lands as a country resort—a pawn by
means of which he can obtain the favour of Buckingham.

But the moral problems of the age are presented at the highest
level in the character of James. To most readers, aware that
James is a comic figure from beginning to end, the suggestion
that he might have more than merely a comic significance may
constitute an attempt to spoil the fun. This objection certainly
gains force when we examine the final scene, in which James
bestows the accolade on Richie, dubbing him Sir Richard
Moniplies of Castle Collup, and then leads his court away to
the cock-a-leekie. Here Scott, in the liveliest and most adroit
conclusion of the entire Waverley series, is treating one of
James's most conspicuously decadent policies as a source of

35 *F.N.*, ch. 10.   36 *Ibid.*

innocent merriment. Yet if Scott, in presenting James, is too much entertained by him to become solemn, he is also too well aware of James' position in history to allow the reader to forget about it. Hence the undercurrent of pathos in the scene during which James instructs Heriot in the proper way to present petitions :

> " By my halidome," said the King, " ye are a ceevileezed fellow, Geordie, and I carena if I fling awa as much time as may teach ye. And, first, see you, sir, ye shall approach the presence of majesty thus—shadowing your eyes with your hand, to testify that you are in the presence of the vicegerent of Heaven. Vera weel, George, that is done in a comely manner. Then, sir, ye sall kneel, and make as if you would kiss the hem of our garment, the latch of our shoe, or such-like. Very weel enacted. Whilk we, as being willing to be debonair and pleasing towards our lieges, prevent thus—and motion to you to rise ; whilk, having a boon to ask, as yet you obey not, but, gliding your hand into your pouch, bring forth your supplication, and place it reverentially in our open palm." [37]

It is clear from this that James has nothing but pedantry and conceit with which to oppose the general drift toward laxity in the observance of court ceremonies. It is also clear why Allan Nevins could assert without qualification that no historian has ever equalled Scott in his portrait of James.[38]

Another characteristic of James which Scott emphasises is his Christian and humanitarian opposition to both national and private warfare. Thus he defends the Ramsay pedigree against the scorn of Sir Mungo Malagrowther :

> " Heard ye never of Sir William Ramsay of Dalwolsey, man, of whom John Fordoun saith, ' He was *bellicosissimus, nobilissimus* ? ' His castle stands to witness for itsell, not

---

[37] *F.N.*, ch. 5.
[38] A. Nevins, *The Gateway to History*, revised edn., Chicago 1962, p. 397.

three miles from Dalkeith, man, and within a mile of
Bannockrig. Davie Ramsay came of that auld and
honoured stock, and I trust he hath not derogated from
his ancestors by his present craft. They all wrought wi'
steel, man ; only the auld knights drilled holes wi' their
swords in their enemies' corslets, and he saws nicks in
his brass wheels. And I hope it is as honourable to give
eyes to the blind as to slash them out of the head of those
that see ; and to show us how to value our time as it
passes, as to fling it away in drinking, brawling, spear-
splintering, and such-like unchristian doings." [39]

There is a note of burlesque in this, as well as the implication
that James's renunciation of ancient practice is a sign that the
world grows older rather than better. Moreover, Scott reports
elsewhere that James's pre-natal " exposure " to Rizzio's murder
was thought to have given him a neurotic bias against violence.[40]
Thus Scott's recurrent theme of pacifism and non-violence
achieves a decidedly individual and eccentric embodiment.

But there is one subject about which Scott admits no am-
bivalence. James appears at his weakest and most contemptible
when he endeavours, after Huntinglen has seconded Nigel's petition in his usual blunt manner, to belittle the value of Nigel's land :

" To grant the truth," he said . . . " this is a hard case ;
and harder than it was represented to me, though I had
some inkling of it before. And so the lad only wants
payment of the siller due from us, in order to reclaim his
paternal estate ? But then, Huntinglen, the lad will have
other debts, and why burden himsell with sae mony acres
of barren woodland ? Let the land gang, man—let the
land gang. Steenie has the promise of it from our
Scottish chancellor : it is the best hunting-ground in
Scotland ; and Baby Charles and Steenie want to kill a
buck there this next year. They maun hae the land—
they maun hae the land ; and our debt shall be paid to
the young man plack and bawbee, and he may have the

[39] *F.N.*, ch. 37.   [40] *F.N.*, ch. 27.

spending of it at our court; or if he has such an eard
hunger, wouns ! man, we'll stuff his stomach with English
land, which is worth twice as much, ay, ten times as
much, as these accursed hills and heughs, and mosses and
muirs, that he is sae keen after." [41]

Everything in this speech—the timid concern over the
desires of Buckingham and the Prince, the lack of fellow-feeling
for Nigel as a Scot, above all the slight opinion of the value of
land, as well as the consideration of that value as an exclusively
economic one without additions resulting from its poetic and
associative connexions with the past—indicates degeneration on
on the part of James. In *The Heart of Midlothian* Scott had
shown a queen who, in granting Jeanie's petition, had revealed
herself, for a moment at least, in a realm where political injustice
or historical decay could not reach her. But James' response to
Nigel's petition is the answer of a king who belongs far too much
to a single time, the present, where expediency exerts the greatest
pressure.

Such implicit judgments may be condemned as routine
Toryism—a return to the ethical simplicities of *Guy Mannering*.
Nevertheless, in *The Fortunes of Nigel* virtue and ambiguity are
not seen as synonymous at all times and on all levels. When, in
his 1831 introduction, Scott contrasts " the ancient rough and
wild manners of a barbarous age " with " the illumination of increased or revived learning and the instructions of renewed or
reformed religion," he sounds partial to change. Moreover, his
reference to the " quixotic dictates " of chivalry and his praise
of Bacon hardly set the proper tone for a novel in which vice is
often linked with innovation. And the novel itself, although its
general ideological bias is clear enough, is no seamless texture of
neo-feudal convictions. The thoroughly virtuous Heriot looks
upon traditional virtues as an outsider and as one who is of the
new world, not the old ; even James's attack upon chivalric spear-
splintering is a cogent expression of both Baconian and middle-
class philosophy ; and Huntinglen, who carries with him the

[41] *F.N.*, ch. 9.

memory of ancient traditions in all their purity, expresses satisfaction that the days of feudal violence are at an end.[42]

Such complexities add richness to a novel already rich in its own distinctive virtues. These virtues include the superb and atmospheric descriptions of interiors; the suggestion, particularly in the Whitefriars scenes, of a labyrinthine and dangerous city— an effect that looks back to Shadwell and Jonson and forward to Dickens; the charming and subtly allusive imitations of Jacobean drama in the handling of such scenes as the interview between Ursula Suddlechop and Margaret Ramsay in Ch. 8 (the scene ends, appropriately, with Margaret's soliloquy!); and the thoroughly successful blend of pathos and comedy in the character of James.

I confess, however, that these benefits are more meaningful to me because of my bias in favour of those works of Scott that concern " the opposition of ancient manners to those which are gradually subduing them." This element of dynamic process in the enveloping social world is a force which adds depth and credibility to the characters who must make their way in such a world. Even the black villainy of Dalgarno is more believable than the histrionics of Prince John because it has its objective correlative, not only in his greed, but also in his amoral determination to keep up-to-date.

Thus, to bring matters to a point, *The Fortunes of Nigel* succeeds because it possesses so much in common with the novels of a changing Scotland.

[42] *F.N.*, ch. 10.

IO

ST RONAN'S WELL

> " Hence it follows, that though a good acting play
> may be made by selecting a plot and characters
> from a novel, yet scarce any effort of genius
> could render a play into a narrative romance."
>
> — Scott, " Henry Fielding "

The accepted view that the novels of modern Scotland are the best of the Waverley series is fortunately not dependent upon *St Ronan's Well*. Coming after *Quentin Durward* it seems as wrong as a novel can be—structurally confused and improbable, awkward in style and tone, and trivial in effect.

Its most obvious flaw is renowned as an example of Ballantyne's aggressive Grundyism and Scott's lack of aesthetic courage. The central plot concerns the triangular relationship between Clara Mowbray and the half-brothers Francis Tyrrel and Valentine Bulmer. In the past Tyrrel loved Clara and won her consent to marriage, but since a fortune was to be inherited by the son who married into the ancient Mowbray family, Bulmer substituted himself for Tyrrel at the wedding. When the deception was discovered, Clara was naturally unsettled, but since the mock-marriage had not been consummated the reader may wonder why her mind became permanently clouded by near-insanity. The answer is well known. Scott had intended that Clara be vulnerable to shock because she had already given herself to

Tyrrel before the ceremony with Bulmer. Ballantyne, however, acting as the representative of a presumably over-sensitive reading public, objected strenuously to the idea of a gentlewoman misbehaving before marriage, and Scott let him have his way and suppressed the fact of Clara's prior indiscretion.[1]

Obviously Scott's failure to resist Ballantyne was a crime against the laws of fiction. One could hardly imagine *The Heart of Midlothian* without Effie's transgression, and Clara's mad remorse requires an equally significant deviation.

Nevertheless, had Scott stuck to his guns he would not have saved *St Ronan's Well*, for the plot he chose was totally unsuited to his medium. The principal sources of Scott's story were dramatic. The use of a spa as a background for social and erotic competition was suggested by *The Rivals*, and Captain McTurk, who goes about making trouble by arranging duels, resembles Sheridan's Lucius O'Trigger. But the most important source, as the hostile critic of the *Monthly Review* pointed out, was Otway's *The Orphan*.[2] Scott admired Otway,[3] and although the device of the disguised bride or bridegroom was part of the joint-stock of the Restoration dramatists, Otway's treatment of it is closest in detail and in pathetic feeling to the situation in *St Ronan's Well*. There is the same triangle of a woman and two brothers, the same deception at the wedding, the same remorse on the part of the heroine, exhibited in a tendency toward distracted wandering, and the same honourable surrender of rights by her real lover. Scott changes the motivation of one of the

---

[1] Lockhart says (IV. 151-2) that " Miss Mowbray's mock marriage had not halted at the profane ceremony of the church," but J. M. Collyer, using the original proofs, demonstrated that Scott's intentions were those summarised above. See " The ' Catastrophe ' in ' St Ronan's Well ' ", in *The Athenaeum*, (1893), pp. 154-5. I must admit that I find Mr F. R. Hart's attempt (*Scott's Novels*, pp. 275-86) to demonstrate the possible truth of both accounts very tenuous.

[2] *The Monthly Review*, CIII (1824), pp. 61-75.

[3] " Essay on the Drama ", in *The Miscellaneous Prose Works of Sir Walter Scott, Bart.*, 28 vols., Edinburgh 1851-7, vi. 356. See also Alice Mackenzie Taylor, *Next to Shakespeare : Otway's " Venice Preserv'd " and " The Orphan "* ..., Durham (N.C.) 1950, p. 263.

principals by making Bulmer a fortune-hunter rather than a sincere rival in love, but the change does not effect the articulation of the story.

Scott could hardly have committed a worse strategic blunder than to borrow from Otway. The success of *The Orphan* would demand the acceptance of highly artificial theatrical conventions. Among these is the assumption that a reasonably intelligent person can carry off a disguise under almost any circumstances. Another is that human emotions are supple enough to adjust with relative ease to the discoveries and reversals of a mechanistic plot. Scott, however, was writing a realistic novel—long and generously explanatory. The spirit of every paragraph makes war against our believing that Bulmer succeeded in carrying off his mock-marriage because of the darkness of the church, that young as he was, he went through with his plans without wondering whether the marriage was binding for the purposes of inheritance,[4] that, as originally intended, Hannah Irwin set Tyrrel and Clara together merely because, having been herself deflowered, she was resentful of virginity as such. In *Waverley*, *Old Mortality*, and *The Heart of Midlothian* Scott had, by his grasp of social and political fact, brought new ideas of motivation into the novel. In *St Ronan's Well* the motivations are dated and transferred by force from one medium into another; hence the bustle of the narrative seems finally causeless.

Nowhere is the question of motivation more crucial than in the behaviour of Tyrrel. One of Scott's persistent excesses is his tendency to overdo the motive of honourable self-denial. Reasonably handled, this theme can ennoble a Jeanie Deans. At other times, as in the last chapters of *Old Mortality*, it puzzles and invites speculation. But in *St Ronan's Well*, even when we reconstruct the pre-Ballantyne version, Tyrrel's determination to leave Clara seems nothing more than a sort of high-minded caddishness. To avoid her for the sake of her own peace of mind—Tyrrel's stated motive[5]—could only be considered an adequate response to her desperation if the real emotional grounds of such a decision are presented. But the abortive conversation

[4] *S.R.W.*, ch. 26.   [5] *S.R.W.*, ch. 29.

between a distracted Clara and her tongue-tied former lover, their only extended exchange in the novel, hardly constitutes such a presentation. The Cavalier poet Lovelace offered his Lucasta a clear-cut alternative—love or honour. Tyrrel rejects both, even though to stay beside Clara, if only to minister quietly to a mind diseased, would have been a decent course. Instead, he becomes a hovering memory during the concluding chapters (like the despised Lovel of *The Antiquary*) and when Clara is dead, he enters a Moravian mission, " for the use of which he had previously drawn considerable sums." [6]

Tyrrel's behaviour suggests that in *St Ronan's Well* Scott was pursuing negativism for its own sake. Not even Peregrine Touchwood, the self-appointed *bourgeois* saviour of ancient patrimonies, escapes the general debility. He enters the novel full of good intentions, but degenerates into a busy fool, condemned for playing Sir Politick Would-be in the affairs of others. When we last hear of him he is " forming plans which have no object, and accumulating a fortune, for which he has apparently no heir." [7] There is some hope that Mowbray will be his inheritor, but Mowbray himself is a reformed gambler who has embraced the opposite extreme of parsimony. His future, at best, is narrow.

Perhaps the best way to understand *St Ronan's Well* is to regard it as an attempt to impose the spirit of *The Bride of Lammermoor* upon refractory materials. If *A Legend of Montrose* is included, nine novels intervene between the two works. But the time elapsed measured only about five years, and when Scott touched home ground again the song of Lucy still rang in his ears. Once again an ancient family is cursed by political hard luck and suffers inevitable decline,[8] and again its estate is surrounded by a modern parody of its ancient community of dependents. Even the theme of a kingless Israel has its faint echo in the absence of a Beau Nash to preside over the idlers at the spa.[9] Clara, despite her aping of Diana Vernon's transvestitism, is much closer to Lucy Ashton in her frustration in

---

[6] *S.R.W.*, ch. 39.   [7] *Ibid.*   [8] *S.R.W.*, ch. 1.
[9] *S.R.W.*, ch. 3.

love, her madness, and her violent end. Mowbray, like Edgar Ravenswood, has his back to the wall, and must gamble for his estate. Like Edgar, he is embarrassed by poverty when confronted with the prospect of visitors, and he is contemptuous of his guests when they depart, a strange recurrence of a theme, considering Scott's deserved reputation as one of the first hosts of Europe. Near the end of the novel there appears a paragraph which, given a change in character relationships, could have been inserted in *The Bride* without detection :

He held out his hand, and she placed, but not without reluctant terror, her trembling palm in his. In this manner, and with a sort of mournful solemnity, as if they had been in attendance upon a funeral, he handed his sister through a gallery hung with old family pictures, at the end of which was Clara's bedchamber. The moon, which at this moment looked out through a huge volume of mustering clouds that had long been boding storm, fell on the two last descendants of that ancient family, as they glided hand in hand, more like the ghosts of the deceased than like living persons, through the hall and amongst the portraits of their forefathers. The same thoughts were in the breast of both, but neither attempted to say, while they cast a flitting glance on the pallid and decayed representations, " How little did these anticipate this catastrophe of their house ! "[10]

The resemblances between *The Bride* and *St Ronan's Well* are significant. Scott, as popular author, was always hopeful of breaking new ground.[11] But in Scotland it would appear that there is no new ground to break. Were it not for the intervening novels the two would probably be regarded as a pair of novels of misery, one with a plot adequate as an " objective correlative " and one without. We can accept the relationship between erotic and social failure in *The Bride*, especially when the vicious Lady Ashton spins the plot, but not in a novel based upon bowdlerised Otway.

[10] *S.R.W.*, ch. 35.   [11] *Journal*, I. 249.

Nor does *St Ronan's Well* offer much in the way of peripheral benefits. Scott's famous commendation of *Pride and Prejudice* reserves the " bow-wow strain " for himself and leaves pointed social observation to Jane Austen.[12] It is a fine example of candour, and it may reflect the experience of writing *St Ronan's Well*. The idlers at the spa are overdrawn ; this is no great flaw, since the Jonson-Smollett view of character portrayal was perfectly valid even before Dickens began to make his own use out of it. The real problem with Scott's handling of Sir Bingo Binks, Mr Winterblossom, Lady Penelope Penfeather, and their colleagues is that he lacks a valid medium for his own satirical language. Arnold Kettle may be right when he finds in both Jane Austen and much of Scott a shared assumption of fixed values that reveals itself in " secure and confident rhythms, binding together words used with a precise social significance," [13] but we have seen enough of Scott's indecision to know that an insecurity in the posture of judgment is one of his most common traits. And when this insecurity is combined with a natural diffidence in the presence of even a shadow of the *beau monde* the result is disastrous. The style of Jane Austen, even in the simplest paragraph of narration, is itself a background of poised and classic judgment against which folly need only to appear in order to be exposed. The *St Ronan's* style, with its half-hearted mock-heroic intentions, offers no such criterion. Two passages, separated by only a few pages, will illustrate :

> " A choir of Dryads and Naiads, assembled at the healing spring of St. Ronan's, have learned with surprise that a youth, gifted by Apollo, when the Deity was prodigal, with two of his most esteemed endowments, wanders at will among their domains, frequenting grove and river, without once dreaming of paying homage to its tutelary deities." [14]

[12] *Op. cit.*, I. 135.
[13] A. Kettle, *An Introduction to the English Novel*, 2 vols., New York 1960, I. 105.
[14] *S.R.W.* ch. 15.

Not only had the assistance of the Scottish Themis, so propitiously indulgent to the foibles of the fair, been resorted to on the occasion, but even Mars seemed ready to enter upon the tapis, if Hymen had not intervened. There was, *de par le monde*, a certain brother of the lady. . . .[15]

The first passage was written by Mr Chatterly, the silly social divine, in his letter to Tyrrel. The second was written by the author.

Had Scott maintained a rigorous, no-nonsense stylistic point of view he might well have chosen that of the poised masculine intelligence, resisting the inanities of female affectation. There is one remarkable passage in which, despite Ballantyne and Mrs Grundy, he manages a touch of barrack-room humour. Lady Penelope has been plaguing Tyrrel for a copy of his sketches :

" I really have little that could possibly be worth the attention of such a judge as your ladyship," answered Tyrrel ; " such trifles as your ladyship has seen I some-times leave at the foot of the tree I have been sketching."

" As Orlando left his verses in the Forest of Ardennes ? Oh, the thoughtless prodigality ! Mr. Winterblossom, do you hear this ? We must follow Mr. Tyrrel in his walks, and glean what he leaves behind him."

Her ladyship was here disconcerted by some laughter on Sir Bingo's side of the table, which she chastised by an angry glance. . . .[16]

Sir Bingo, be it remembered, was a sportsman and a follower of game.

The passage, however, is exceptional. Despite a certain ease and colloquial gusto in the letters and conversations of men like Etherington and Mowbray, Scott has no firm base in *St Ronan's Well*. In choosing his subject he has walked into a quicksand. The contemporary world offered matter enough for his concern over historical change, but his mind, as *The Antiquary* revealed,

[15] *S.R.W.*, ch. 6.   [16] *Ibid.*

required a certain distancing and perspective in order to compose his preoccupations into a valid fictional order. Perhaps this need explains the rather wistful slip of the pen that occurs in his account of Bulmer-Etheridge's bad habits: " He had been a duellist, the manners of the age authorized it. . . ." [17] As if the period of the Peninsular Wars had to be recalled from the mists of antiquity !

Two interesting features of *St Ronan's Well* remain to be noted. One of them can best be regarded as an informal experiment in *leitmotif*. The earlier chapters in particular are saturated with man-beast imagery. The centre of this image system is the mind of Clara, and the psychological appropriateness for one who has been victimised by lust and greed needs no amplification :

> " Bring Lady Binks, if she has the condescension to honour us . . . bring Mr. Springblossom—Winterblossom —and all the lions and lionesses ; we have room for the whole collection. My brother, I suppose, will bring his own particular regiment of bears, which, with the usual assortment of monkeys seen in all caravans, will complete the menagerie." [18]

Such beast imagery is not confined to Clara; it recurs throughout the novel and anticipates the recurrence of the hand imagery in *The Fair Maid of Perth*.[19]

Finally, there is the innkeeper Meg Dods. Meg is a traditionalist whose parents were favourite servants of the Mowbrays. She knows history only as a process of decay, substituting suburban blight for feudal stability. There is a peculiarly contemporary quality in her difficulties. The highroad has been deflected, causing a decline in custom, and the new hotel flourishes at her expense.[20] But she refuses to become obsolete and carries on her chores at the Cleikum Inn with a perpetual dedicated rage. She is unable to wield a broom without implying a criticism of

[17] *S.R.W.*, ch. 33.   [18] *S.R.W.*, ch. 7.
[19] F. R. Hart, " *The Fair Maid . . .*", *passim*.
[20] *S.R.W.*, ch. 1.

" the present, ignorant time," and her speech has a unique
headlong force :

" But my Leddy Penelope Penfeather had fa'an ill, it's
like, as nae other body ever fell ill, and sae she was to be
cured some gate naebody was ever cured, which was
naething mair than was reasonable ; and my leddy, ye ken,
has wit at wull, and has a' the wise folk out from Edinburgh, at her house at Windywa's yonder, which it is her
leddyship's wull and pleasure to call Air Castle ; and they
have a' their different turns, and some can clink verses wi'
their tale as weel as Rob Burns or Allan Ramsay ; and
some rin up hill and down dale, knapping the chucky
stanes to pieces wi' hammers, like sae mony road-makers
run daft—they say it is to see how the warld was made !
—and some that play on all manner of ten-stringed
instruments ; and a wheen sketching souls, that ye may see
perched like craws on every craig in the country, e'en
working your ain trade, Maister Francie ; forbye men that
had been in foreign parts, or said they had been there,
whilk is a' ane, ye ken ; and maybe twa or three draggle-
tailed misses, that wear my Leddy Penelope's follies
when she has dune wi' them, as her queans of maids wear
her second-hand claithes. So, after leddyship's happy
recovery, as they ca'd it, down cam the haill tribe of
wild geese, and settled by the Well, to dine thereout on
the bare grund, like a wheen tinklers ; and they had sangs,
and tunes, and healths, nae doubt, in praise of the
fountain, as they ca'd the Well, and of Leddy Penelope
Penfeather ; and, lastly, they behoved a' to take a solemn
bumper of the spring, which, as I'm tauld, made unco
havoc amang them or they wan hame ; and this they ca'd
picknick, and a plague to them ! And sae the jig was
begun after her leddyship's pipe, and mony a mad
measure has been danced sin' syne ; for down cam masons
and murgeon-makers, and preachers and player-folk,
and Episcopalians and Methodists, and fools and fiddlers,

and Papists and pie-bakers, and doctors and drugsters,
bye the shop-folk, that sell trash and trumpery at three
prices ; and so up got the bonny new Well, and down fell
the honest auld town of St. Ronan's, where blythe decent
folk had been heartsome eneugh for mony a day before
ony o' them were born, or ony sic vapouring fancies
kittled in their cracked brains." [21]

Meg demonstrates, however, not only that a well-realised
character cannot save a novel, but that it can even be disastrous.
In the passage above Meg manages to say all that Scott said in
his careful efforts to dramatise the follies of the spa visitors.
Nowhere else in *St Ronan's Well* is the affectation, the trivial
formalism, the meaningless cosmopolitanism of these fraudulent
sophisticates so well illustrated. We have seen that the sanity
of the peasantry and the idiocy of their " betters " is one of
Scott's favourite themes, but in order to be effective the contrast
must have some balance and tension between the character and
commitments of the aristocrats and the vigorous natural wisdom
of the peasants. Meg, on the other hand, gets the better of
everyone, including Scott. No wonder his introduction, written
late in life for the collected edition, sounds so weary and apolo-
getic. It indirectly confirms his earlier confession to Ballantyne
concerning *Redgauntlet* : " I never liked St. Ronan's—this I
think better of. . . ." [22]

---

[21] *S.R.W.*, ch. 2.

[22] *Letters*, VIII. 20. See also the generally negative view in *Journal*,
I. 207.

I I

REDGAUNTLET

"Of all schools commend me to the Stoicks."

— Scott's *Journal*

It is not difficult to distinguish and define the special qualities of Scott's last major Scottish novel: arbitrariness, eccentricity, and a strong impression of having been composed to please the author rather than the public or the critics. Having written of the Jacobites in *Waverley* and *Rob Roy*, and having noted their activities wherever they appeared in his other novels, Scott returns to them once more, even to the extent of bringing Charles Stuart back to the British Isles years after the '45.

For a world-renowned author whose footsteps were being dogged by a host of critics ready to mark every mis-step—every "falling off"—such a move was bound to provoke hostile comment. "We are tired . . . of the Jacobites," said the *Monthly Review*, and the *New Monthly* shared this opinion.[1] Since neither critic saw what Scott was really up to, these reactions can be understood. But the *Westminster Review* went too far: ". . . the genius of the author of *Waverley* has degenerated to the ordinary slip-slop of the circulating library." [2] On the contrary,

[1] *The Monthly Review*, CLV (1824), p. 200 ; *The New Monthly Magazine and Literary Journal*, II (1824) pp. 94-5.
[2] *The Westminster Review*, II (1824), p. 180.

Miss Buskbody was never farther from his thoughts, and what some considered warmed-over porridge is something entirely different—a reworking of the theme of historical renunciation by a man who had returned the errant Edward Waverley to prose and sanity only to raise up in later works a devil of black nostalgia that refused to be exorcised.

Nor was Scott arbitrary only in his choice of subject. In his Scottish novels he had always exhibited a considerable deference to historical fact. In *Redgauntlet* such deference is very nearly absent. We know, of course, that Charles's visit to Britain in 1745 was not his last, and that the Elibank plot was a thoroughly serious undertaking.[3] Moreover, in emphasizing the troublesome issue of Clementina Walkinshaw, Charles' supposedly treacherous mistress, Scott was on firm historical ground.[4]

Nevertheless, *Redgauntlet* has no sustained relevance to any real historical event. It takes place in the mid-1760s, over ten years after the suspected Clementina had left Charles for ever, and it ignores (except in the Introduction) the distinctive feature of the Elibank plot—its dependence upon a *coup d'état* in London.[5] As for Charles, Scott describes him as having lost " the elasticity of limb and of spirit which had, twenty years before, carried him over many a Highland hill, as light as one of their native deer." [6] The description is tactful, for by the mid-1760s Charles had very nearly become a " Driv'ler and a Show," exhibiting his drunkenness before disapproving Continentals.[7]

Another indication of the creatively gratuitous nature of *Redgauntlet* is the element of personal reminiscence found in the earlier epistolary chapters. Lockhart, as we have seen, convincingly identifies Saunders Fairford with Scott's father.[8] He

[3] C. Petrie, *The Jacobite Movement : The Last Phase*, London 1950, pp. 140-59.

[4] Petrie, *op. cit.*, p. 149. Petrie even indicates (pp. 173-4) that Scott had access to documents, since lost, proving the existence of an interesting proposal to raise the Chevalier's standard in the insurgent American colonies.

[5] Petrie, *op. cit.*, pp. 144-7.   [6] *R.*, ch. 23.

[7] Petrie, *The Jacobite Movement*, p. 175.

[8] Lockhart, I. 161-3, 166.

also believes that Alan Fairford is Scott and that Darsie Latimer is William Clerk.[9] The assumption, while persuasive, would in no way contradict the meaningful possibility that Darsie and Alan are simply two opposing sides of Scott himself, a final realisation of the dualism that set Edward Waverley against Talbot and Morton against Evandale. This opposition is always tempered by affection: ". . . my love for Alan Fairford surpasses the love of woman," writes Darsie.[10] But we know that Scott loved the rebel within himself and allowed him considerable freedom of operation.

The clearest evidence, however, that *Redgauntlet* comes from what Edwin Muir called Scott's " inner world "[11] is that element of sheer wilfulness in plotting, motivation, and narrative method that makes *Redgauntlet* a study of the extremes of violence and pacifism, fanaticism and cowardice, historical damnation and salvation. Scott's last full-length Scottish novel contains a vision of Hell, a picture of an earthly Paradise, a deed of ultimate Quixotic folly, a visitation of overwhelming and unexpected royal grace, and a concluding " Amen."

The novel begins with thirteen epistolary chapters—an exchange between Darsie Latimer and Alan Fairford. Darsie is in the West, exploring the area around the Solway Firth and wondering who he really is. Alan is in Edinburgh, beginning his destined career in the law. Their prose styles, as one reviewer complained, are indistinguishable.[12] Of course they are, for both are young men of reasonably sound, and recent, schooling, and both indulge in the verbal exhibitionism of collegiate table-talk. Nevertheless their badinage has point, for their letters are actually an antiphon of loving but divergent temperaments. Darsie is a romantic of " high and heroic dreams," aspiring after " the Lord knows what." The words are the dutiful Alan's, who, in the same passage associates his friend's ambitions with "some Gothic throne, rough with barbaric pearl and gold."[13] On the other

---

[9] Lockhart, I. 143.   [10] *R.*, Letter 12.

[11] E. Muir, *Scott and Scotland : The Predicament of the Scottish Writer*, New York 1938, p. 150.

[12] *The Monthly Review*, CLV (1824), p. 200.   [13] *R.*, Letter 2.

hand, Darsie's view of Alan's future is a dismal one : " By my faith, man, I could as soon think of being one of those ingenious traders who cheat little Master Jackies on the outside of the partition with tops, balls, bats, and battledores as a member of the long-robed fraternity within, who impose on grown country gentlemen with bouncing brocards of law." [14]   They are devoted friends, and each has some of the qualities of the other, but the reader could easily imagine them carrying on their amiable quarrel to the end of their lives.   Scott's very success in capturing the tone of late adolescent banter may be deceptive, for their differences are no more to be taken lightly than those between Elinor and Marianne Dashwood or Elizabeth and Jane Bennet. Moreover, by the time their exchange of letters is finished Scott has left the reader in a quandary.   He may justly suspect that Darsie is the true " hero " of the novel, but how is he to be sure ? Scott maintains the balance so well that the novel goes on for pages without a formal character-centre.

Moreover, if the Alan-Darsie divergence is to be taken seriously, the same must be said of the complexity of attitudes concerning Saunders Fairford.   Scott completes his long succession of troubled father-son relationships with a portrait of " the thing itself "—a man whose perfectly honourable and dutiful Philistinism is exactly calculated to induce filial rebellion and filial shame.   Once Scott's own father becomes a secondary character in a novel he can be studied, analysed, and controlled by the new " father "—the creator and manipulator of the fiction. The result, however, is no mere head-over-heels reversal of family order, for not only is Alan Fairford reasonably respectful, but the rebellious side of him is partly accounted for by Darsie. And when, having abandoned both the epistolary method and Darsie's Journal as narrative devices, Scott assumes the stance of the omniscient author, the respectfulness continues.

Nevertheless, certain clear oppositions remain, and they are undeniable.   Here is Alan's account of his father's behaviour when he had discovered that the two friends had taken an excursion together :

[14] *R.*, Letter I.

My boots encountered his first glance of displeasure, and he asked me, with a sneer, which way I had been riding. He expected me to answer, "Nowhere," and would then have been at me with his usual sarcasm, touching the humour of walking in shoes at twenty shillings a pair. But I answered with composure that I had ridden out to dinner as far as Noble House. He started . . . as if I had said that I had dined at Jericho; and as I did not choose to seem to observe his surprise, but continued munching my radishes in tranquillity, he broke forth in ire.

"To Noble House, sir! and what had you to do at Noble House, sir? Do you remember you are studying law, sir? that your Scots law trials are coming on, sir? that every moment of your time just now is worth hours at another time? and have you leisure to go to Noble House, sir? and to throw your books behind you for so many hours? Had it been a turn in the Meadows, or even a game at golf—but Noble House, sir!" [15]

This is heavy-handed, and the image of a sneering father and a son disdainfully muching radishes conveys no impression of harmony. Scott softens the scene in succeeding paragraphs by displaying some of Saunders' more charitable impulses toward Darsie, but there is still no doubt that his view of that young hero is tinged with contempt:

"It is very true," he said, "Darsie was a pleasant companion; but over waggish—over waggish, Alan, and somewhat scatter-brained. . . . But Darsie, as I was saying, is an arch lad, and somewhat light in the upper story. I wish him well through the world; but he has little solidity, Alan—little solidity." [16]

He then goes on to accuse Darsie of idle habits, with another passing sneer for his son, and finally he packs him off to his law-books.

[15] *R.*, Letter 2.   [16] *Ibid.*

L

Alan continues his account with a paragraph of mingled praise and complaint :

> Latimer, I will tell you no lies. I wish my father would allow me a little more exercise of my free will, were it but that I might feel the pleasure of doing what would please him of my own accord. A little more spare time, and a little more money to enjoy it, would, besides, neither misbecome my age nor my condition ; and it is, I own, provoking to see so many in the same situation winging the air at freedom, while I sit here, caged up like a cobbler's linnet, to chant the same un-varied lesson from sunrise to sunset, not to mention the listening to so many lectures against idleness, as if I enjoyed or was making use of the means of amusement ! But then I cannot at heart blame either the motive or the object of this severity.[17]

Alan is indeed telling no lies, either in his complaints or in his final reconciliatory sentence. But he later delivers judgment both against his father and his precious law in the most emphatic way possible. The locally famous case of Peebles v. Plainstanes is his father's choice for his first legal effort. This case, anticipating in its muddled complexity Dickens's more notorious Jarndyce and Jarndyce, is no credit to Peebles, Plainstanes, or the law itself. And when Alan, in the midst of his plea before the Bench, accidentally discovers a letter informing him that Darsie has vanished in the West of Scotland, he throws up the case, runs out of the court, and abandons both Peebles and his father. Nor is his melodramatic exit without a certain poetic justice, since Saunders knew of the letter and had tried to keep it concealed from his son.[18]

What happens to Saunders after this crisis is interesting. He repents his deceit, covers up as well as possible for his son's sudden flight, reflects bitterly on the character of Darsie, and scolds his servants unmercifully until " the acrimonious humours

---

[17] *R.*, Letter 2.   [18] *Ibid.*

settled in a hissing-hot fit of the gout ... under whose discipline we shall, for the present, leave him...." But why "for the present"? Saunders Fairford never reappears. His son and his son's other self are left to seek each other in the West, among fiddlers, dancers, drunkards, spies, Quakers, and Jacobites. Even in the final scenes at Joe Crackenthorp's inn, where Scott marshals his important characters for a climactic ensemble, the senior Fairford is conspicuously absent.

As for Darsie's own adventures, they carry him into a world both violent and obscure. His first significant encounter is with the incoming tide of the Solway Firth, which nearly costs him his life. The Solway tides are a dominant image in *Redgauntlet*, and however much Scott's use of them may owe to his son-in-law's *Reginald Dalton*,[19] they exist on their own as Scott's most provocative symbol of historical process. The tides are irresistible, dangerous, and, above all, cyclical. They suggest a view of reality more Stoic than Hegelian, and they hardly encourage a belief in progress. They are not to be controlled by the will of man, although they can be observed and, in some cases, employed in prudent passivity. But when Darsie is rescued by Redgauntlet he encounters a man whose popular title, "Laird of the Solway Lakes," takes on ironic overtones as the novel moves forward. For Redgauntlet is a man of violence determined to command the tides of history or die in the effort. His sense of past and present is dominated by a legitimist fanaticism and a sense of family doom that defies the laws of nature and history both.[20] It is his belief, itself a parody of historical cyclicism, that the Redgauntlets are fated to draw the sword everlastingly in lost causes, and it is this inheritance of valiant social masochism that he is resolved to transmit to his nephew. Hence he rescues him from the Solway with magnificent courage and skill[21] in order to devote him to death.

The Westminster Review offers its own contemptuous comment on Redgauntlet's subsequent treatment of Darsie: "He knocks his nephew on the head, puts him in a cage, locks him up,

[19] *The Westminster Review*, II (1824), pp. 193-4.
[20] *R.*, ch. 8.   [21] *Ibid.*

threatens to blow his brains out, canters him over the country in petticoats, with his head in an iron mask, and then asks him to oblige his loving uncle so far as to put his neck into a halter for a prince for whom he did not care two straws." [22] The reviewer seems unaware of the possible desperation of back-to-the-wall reactionaries. Moreover, he could have observed that Redgauntlet's behaviour bears a significant resemblance to that of his ancestor Alberick Redgauntlet, who generations before had ridden over his helpless son in order to get at the Scottish usurper Baliol.[23] The tragedy was commemorated ever after in the horseshoe image on the foreheads of Redgauntlet men. It is the image of the Cavalier, the moss-trooper, the blind clansman or nationalist, and in *Redgauntlet*, the obsolete man determined to make the world stand still.

Despite his violence and hot temper, there can be no doubt that Redgauntlet exercises a mysterious influence over his nephew's feelings. The power comes from personal magnetism and the sense of kinship. It operates, characteristically, in defiance of the law, and Scott dramatises this fact by showing its force when Darsie is brought before Justice Foxley to demand his rights against his uncle's authoritarianism. Foxley is as inept in this minor case as is the Scottish legal system in the case of Peebles vs. Plainstanes. When Redgauntlet, unseen by Foxley, frowns at Darsie to demand recognition, the horseshoe is revealed and Darsie is cowed and defeated.[24] The scene is less noisy than that of Alan's public desertion of Peebles, but the implications are as clear. The law, in its formal and "mechanical" aspects, whether presided over by precisians like Fairford or trimmers like Foxley, is an enemy of power, mystery, blood-consciousness, and even friendship itself.

Nevertheless, Darsie is no willing captive of his uncle. He cannot deny *his* place in history as a child of the post-Jacobite world. Moreover, before his appearance at Foxley's he has undergone two experiences that illuminate the moral dilemmas

---

[22] *The Westminster Review*, II (1824), p. 187.
[23] *R.*, ch. 8.   [24] *R.*, ch. 6.

at the heart of the novel and determine the reader's awareness of his proper role and destiny. One of these is his encounter with the blind fiddler Wandering Willie, the other is his visit with Joshua Geddes.

"Wandering Willie's Tale" can be enjoyed (and anthologised) in its own right, but its place in the novel is no mere distraction. It leads Darsie's imagination into the peculiar hell of which Redgauntlet himself is an emissary. When Willie's "gudesire" Steenie Steenson goes to pay his rent to Sir Robert Redgauntlet, a great harrier of Whigs, he is greeted by the same frown that was later to confront Darsie at Justice Foxley's. Sir Robert dies on the instant, hence Steenie must seek his receipt in Hell, where he encounters a spectacle that indicates clearly the moral stature of factional bitter-enders:

> But, Lord take us in keeping! what a set of ghastly revellers they were that sat round that table! My gudesire kenn'd mony that had long before gane to their place, for often had he piped to the most part in the hall of Redgauntlet. There was the fierce Middleton, and the dissolute Rothes, and the crafty Lauderdale; and Dalyell, with his bald head and a beard to his girdle; and Earlshall, with Cameron's blude on his hand; and wild Bonshaw, that tied blessed Mr. Cargill's limbs till the blude sprung; and Dumbarton Douglas, the twice-turned traitor baith to country and king. There was the Bluidy Advocate MacKenyie, who, for his worldly wit and wisdom, had been to the rest as a god. And there was Claverhouse, as beautiful as when he lived, with his long, dark, curled locks, streaming down over his laced buff-coat, and his left-hand always on his right spule-glade, to hide the wound that the silver bullet had made. He sat apart from them all, and looked at them with a melancholy, haughty countenance; while the rest hallooed, and sung, and laughed, that the room rang. But their smiles were fearfully contorted from time to time; and their laughter passed into such wild sounds as

made my gudesire's very nails grow blue, and chilled the marrow in his banes.[25]

Thus Scott, the Tory and Royalist, fills Hell with red-hot Tories and Royalists. The paradox suits well a writer of such divided emotions as Scott; moreover, the party label matters less than the possible attitudes and styles of life that compete elsewhere in the novel for the loyalty of Darsie.

Among these attitudes the most important is that of Joshua Geddes. Geddes is a Quaker who stands as Scott's most positive symbol of the quietist feelings that found embodiment in Bessie Maclure, Lucy Ashton, and the more passive heroes. Among the more thoroughly developed dissenting figures in the Waverley Novels he is perhaps the most sympathetic. The sympathy is actually enhanced rather than lessened by Scott's awareness of the aggressive impulses that still survive in the man. His temper is " naturally warm and hasty," as his imprecations sometimes demonstrate, but his behaviour under stress reconciles fortitude and pacifism, and Darsie testifies clearly to the impression such behaviour makes upon his own mind.

When Geddes first confronts Redgauntlet in Darsie's presence he receives the traditional Cavalier insults, but Darsie (and Scott) gives the moral predominance to Geddes: "... as they sat fronting each other, I could not help thinking that they might have formed no bad emblem of Peace and War."[26] Moreover, Geddes's faith establishes a Peaceable Kingdom at Mt Sharon, where he and his sister Rachel live in a Franciscan harmony with wild life that mocks the melodrama of violence in which Redgauntlet moves and acts. Scott cannot resist nagging the reader with the awareness that some of Geddes's beasts are being fattened for food, but the doctrinal discomfort that Rachel suffers when Darsie presses her on that matter is to her credit. She neither flares up nor equivocates.[27] Again, the landscaped acres that Darsie surveys represent the eighteenth-century British ideal of tranquil, deferential co-operation with nature in a way that effectively symbolises the simplicity and charity of

[25] *R.,* Letter 11.   [26] *R.,* Letter 6.   [27] *R.,* Letter 7.

the owner. In sheer force of gathered meaning—a meaning made clearer as the novel progresses—Geddes's *locus amoenus* outdoes Fielding's Allworthy estate or Jane Austen's Pemberley. Elsewhere Geddes's way with the resources of nature is both peaceful and rewarding. Others may fish for Solway salmon with spears; Geddes uses tide-nets. His defence of his methods to Darsie includes a rejection of blood-sports (which the romantic Darsie also dislikes), and Darsie pushes him to a distinction between killing for pleasure and killing for a livelihood that Darsie considers " too high-strained." [28] Yet Geddes's nets, when compared with the spears used by Redgauntlet's comrades, offer yet another emblem of Peace against War, with the implication that peace is no less honourable for being the mother of abundance.

The spear-fishers, on the other hand, are noisy, violent, skilful, picturesque, and inefficient. They ride through the shallow Solway waters, chasing the fish " at full gallop . . . as you see hunters spearing boars in the old tapestry." [29] Thus they shed more blood and procure less food than Joshua. Their leader is Redgauntlet, and his presence on the scene, remembered later in the light of his resolution to shed blood all over Britain in order to restore a decadent *roué* to the throne, is ominous. Redgauntlet is to become a fisher of men among troubled waters, his implement is to be the spear, and his nephew must be his comrade-in-arms.

Hence the dialectical appropriateness of the episode in which Darsie is abducted when the Quaker's nets are raided by the spearmen. Darsie's recognition of Geddes's fundamental strength and virtue leads him to accompany him when he goes to face the mob. Scott does not equivocate about Geddes's behaviour at this time. When his watchman shows him two pistols he throws them into a tub of water with a decisiveness that puts any conceivable degree of hypocrisy out of the question. In Joshua's words, " courage is displayed and honour attained . . . by doing and suffering, as becomes a man, that which fate calls us to suffer. . . ." [30] Redgauntlet has other opinions. He is

---

[28] *R.*, Letter 6.   [29] *R.*, Letter 4.   [30] *R.*, ch. 3.

determined to fill the air with noise and the tides with blood on behalf of his own odd conception of fate. His treatment of his nephew, who has " seen " both Claverhouse and Geddes and has, in his presence by the side of Geddes, indicated his choice, must of necessity be arbitrary and, at times, downright silly.

At this point a comparison between *Redgauntlet* and *Waverley* may be illuminating. In his first novel Scott led his hero to the feet of the Pretender with complete deference to the laws of psychological fact and circumstantial probability. If there were mysteries they were later explained by the actions of Fergus MacIvor, Donald Bean Lean, and their operatives. And the " romantic " character of Edward, as well as his natural pride in the face of such inquisitors as Major Melville, were clear motivating forces. Darsie's romantic fancies, on the other hand, are not strong enough to allow a commitment to Charles under any circumstances. He explicitly withholds support from his uncle's cause when presented to the Jacobites at Crackenthorp's, and his later obeisance to Charles is the merest formal gesture.[31] His uncle's only power over him, putting aside sheer physical force, is the sort of personal magnetism he displayed at Foxley's hearing, which can induce a " thrill of awe . . . not unmingled with a wild and mysterious feeling of wonder, almost amounting to pleasure." [32] Such a fleeting and glandular response is not enough.

Hence Redgauntlet must resort to violence and trickery of the most arbitrary kind. His exploits become a persistent and trivial comedy. Darsie is indeed dressed as a woman and cantered about the countryside, and the last Jacobite gesture— the action of a stern and uncompromising fanatic with a tragic dedication—takes on the flavour of *Charley's Aunt*. Never before, unless in the poignant idiocies of Caleb Balderstone, had Scott achieved so ironic a contrast between ideal and reality. Even the Pretender himself behaves like a character in a bedroom farce, disguising himself as " Father Buonaventure " only to be interrupted in a conference with Alan Fairford by the capricious appearance of his mistress.[33]

[31] *R.*, ch. 22.   [32] *R.*, ch. 8.   [33] *R.*, ch. 16.

As for Charles' other assistants, the most respectable of them are indecisive,[34] while the rest belong to Scott's vast gallery of socially obsolete outcasts. Of these the most interesting is Nanty Ewart, a smuggler with very little left to console him but his bottle. Ewart's perceptive comments on the folly of the last Jacobites give the lie for ever to the criticism that Scott without Scots was out of his element:

> " And with whom do you yourself consort, I pray ? "
> replied Nanty. . . . " Why, with plotters, that can make no
> plot to better purpose than their own hanging ; and
> incendiaries, that are snapping the flint upon wet tinder.
> You'll as soon raise the dead as raise the Highlands ;
> you'll as soon get a grunt from a dead sow as any comfort
> from Wales or Cheshire. . . ." [35]

Ewart's own family history is another tragedy of father and son. The father was a Presbyterian minister whose view of his son's first sexual adventure was precisely that of David Deans toward Effie's fall, until he died because of an obviously needless grief. The result of his rigour was predictable—a vagrant, self-torturing alcoholic whose impressive education is wasted in piracy and smuggling and who thinks of himself as a parricide. Alan Fairford's response to Ewart's autobiography is cautious. He may have bolted the court to seek his friend, but, although he pities Ewart, he is " uneasy in his mind at finding himself, a lawyer, so close to a character so lawless. . . ." [36] His reaction here is prophetic of his ultimate acceptance of his professional destiny. If Nanty is a parricide, Alan has brought Saunders little more than an attack of the gout. Nevertheless, one cannot help being amazed at the amount of sheer narrative energy and motivation that Scott finds in the impercipience of fathers.

Ewart's image of wet tinder applies beautifully to the gathering of Redgauntlet's forces at Crackenthorp's. Scott's problem is to dramatise impotence and make stagnation interesting, but his mastery of group psychology in all conceivable moods is

---

[34] *R.*, ch. 22.   [35] *R.*, ch. 14.   [36] *Ibid.*

adequate to the task. We can hardly refrain from pitying Red-gauntlet as he attempts to inspire his " followers " with something like the spirit of Dunois at Burgundy :

> " When the White Standard is again displayed, it shall
> not be turned back so easily, either by the force of its
> enemies or the falsehood of its friends. Doctor Grumball,
> I bow to the representative of Oxford, the mother of
> learning and loyalty. Pengwinion, you Cornish chough,
> has this good wind blown you north ? Ah, my brave
> Cambro-Britons, when was Wales last in the race of
> honour ? "
>
> Such and such-like compliments he dealt around,
> which were in general answered by silent bows ; but
> when he saluted one of his own countrymen by the name
> of MacKellar, and greeted Maxwell of Summertrees by
> that of Pate-in-Peril, the latter replied, " that if Pate were
> not a fool, he would be Pate-in-Safety " ; and the former,
> a thin old gentleman, in tarnished embroidery, said
> bluntly, " Ay, troth, Redgauntlet, I am here just like
> yourself : I have little to lose ; they that took my land the
> last time may take my life this, and that is all I care about
> it."
>
> The English gentlemen, who were still in possession
> of their paternal estates, looked doubtfully on each other,
> and there was something whispered among them of the
> fox which had lost his tail.[37]

These men represent the " drab but necessary progress "[38] against which Redgauntlet fights in vain. All that is needed after such a damp confrontation is the treachery of Christal Nixon to provide the total collapse of Redgauntlet's effort with a circumstantial basis.[39] However, when Nixon betrays the assembled Jacobites to

[37] *R.*, ch. 22.
[38] David Daiches, " Scott's Achievement as a Novelist ", in *Nineteenth-Century Fiction*, VI (1951), p. 84.
[39] *R.*, ch. 23.

the Government, he serves only to justify the course of history by an act of charity, and to allow Redgauntlet to achieve, not the " tedious havoc " of " fabled knights," but the "better fortitude of Patience and Heroic Martyrdom unsung"—for this non-historical figure must reject on his highest possible level of passion and insight that grim adherence to the past that made a Quixotic brute of Fergus MacIvor and a fool out of Caleb Balderstone.

The scene in which this occurs is probably Scott's greatest. Even its gasping repetitions—its confirmations and reconfirmations—are dramatically suited to this moment of reversal. General Campbell, well supported by Hanoverian soldiers, arrives suddenly to demand the dissolution of the conspiracy. But he brings no warrants for death, for the King has assumed his high function as a transcendent force for reconciliation. Campbell simply informs the conspirators, including Charles himself, that they may all withdraw safely to their respective homes without further pursuit or annoyance :

" What !—all ? " exclaimed Sir Richard Glendale— " all, without exception ? "

" ALL, without one single exception," said the General ; " such are my orders. If you accept my terms, say so, and make haste ; for things may happen to interfere with his Majesty's kind purposes towards you all."

" His Majesty's kind purposes ! " said the Wanderer. " Do I hear you aright, sir ? "

" I speak the King's very words, from his very lips," replied the General. " ' I will,' said his Majesty, " deserve the confidence of my subjects by reposing my security in the fidelity of the millions who acknowledge my title —in the good sense and prudence of the few who con-tinue, from the errors of education, to disown it." His Majesty will not even believe that the most zealous Jacobites who yet remain can nourish a thought of exciting a civil war, which must be fatal to their families and themselves, besides spreading bloodshed and ruin through

a peaceful land. He cannot even believe of his kinsman
that he would engage brave and generous, though
mistaken, men in an attempt which must ruin all who
have escaped former calamities ; and he is convinced that,
did curiosity or any other motive lead that person to
visit this country, he would soon see it was his wisest
course to return to the continent ; and his Majesty com-
passionates his situation too much to offer any obstacle
to his doing so."

    " Is this real ? " said Redgauntlet. " Can you mean
this? Am I—are all—are any of these gentlemen at
liberty, without interruption, to embark in yonder brig,
which, I see, is now again approaching the shore ? "

    " You, sir—all—any of the gentlemen present," said
the General—" all whom the vessel can contain, are at
liberty to embark uninterrupted by me ; but I advise none
to go off who have not powerful reasons, unconnected
with the present meeting, for this will be remembered
against no one."

    " Then, gentlemen," said Redgauntlet, clasping his
hands together as the words burst from him, " the cause
is lost for ever ! "[40]

What follows is both moving and credible. Scott, as he had
shown in Jeanie Deans's interview with the Queen, does not
forget the unregenerate facts that intrude upon the noblest
actions. Campbell is anxious and watchful as he accompanies
Charles and Redgauntlet to the waiting boat, Nixon's dead body,
the result of a mutually fatal struggle with Ewart, is a morbid
reminder of the consequences of civil war, and Redgauntlet even
now cannot refrain from a sarcastic comment on the fainthearted-
ness of his followers. Nevertheless, his last words to his nephew
show how far he has travelled in wisdom :

    " The fatal doom . . . will, I trust, now depart from the
    house of Redgauntlet, since its present representative

[40] *R.*, ch. 23.

has adhered to the winning side. I am convinced he will not change it, should it in turn become the losing one."[41]

These last words are realistic and somewhat ambiguous. Redgauntlet still dramatises the concept of loyalty, and he still intends a degree of mastery over Darsie's character. But the desperate grappling with destiny is over both for himself and Darsie, and he knows it. After all his violence, he is capable of this gift of freedom and discreet selfhood.

Intense historical nostalgia is far more than a decorous sentiment, and only a writer who would have fought for the Pretender " to the foot of the gallows "[42] could have properly represented it. But a true assessment of Scott demands the recognition that he was the creator of Geddes as well as Redgauntlet, and it is Geddes's moral vision that is justified in these final scenes. It is fitting that his last exchange with Redgauntlet should draw forth a conciliatory comment from the fanatical spearfisher.[43] Geddes' spiritual calm is the most effective answer to the miseries of historical turmoil, and this calm remains beyond the thrust of historical doom or reversal. At Mt Sharon Geddes had confessed to Darsie that his own ancestors had been as bloody as any others of their day. Yet the predatory armorial symbols on his chimney had been effaced, and Geddes prefers it that way.[44] (Similarly, the horseshoe image has been " effaced " from Darsie's forehead, as he discovers when he indulges in some narcissistic posturing before a mirror.)[45] To Geddes there is grace in acceptance and forgetfulness. All must negotiate somehow with the cyclical movements of human affairs. Even the victorious Campbell, whose message to the conspirators reveals that the King himself shares some of Geddes's wisdom, must allow Redgauntlet's ship to " stay in the offing for a tide."[46]

Scott has been charged with historical fantasy-building, and the charge has a measure of justice. But what are we to make of *Redgauntlet*, where a rebellion that never occurred is defeated by an imagined act of royal forgiveness? For the effect of this is not

[41] *Ibid.*   [42] *Letters*, III. 142.   [43] *R.*, ch. 21.
[44] *R.*, Letter 7.   [45] *R.*, ch. 8.   [46] *R.*, ch. 23.

escapist but realistic in the profoundest sense. Moreover, Scott will not let his characters remain for ever fixed in the postures of noble renunciation. After the " Amen " that resounds from the shore there follows a very brief " Conclusion," in which we learn that Darsie indeed remained loyal to the Hanovers, that Redgauntlet retired to a monastery, pious but not saintly, and that Alan married the charming and elusive " Green Mantle " and settled down as an advocate in the town of " Clinkdollar."

The reader may skip the conclusion if he pleases, but Scott, like Geddes himself, must be forgiven his residue of the old Adam.

human behaviour, is only one source of emotional energy, even in those finally committed to their causes. Mucklewrath attacks Edward apparently because he considers him a dangerous traitor, but he is also goaded by his consciousness that his wife has gotten the better of him in an argument; Melville acts as much from personal *pique* as from official concern for the safety of the realm; and Edward, of course, is in love with Flora MacIvor. The value of such skill in the unforced blending of human and political components cannot be overemphasised. It is true that writers of " The Novel of Doctrine " had brought ideology into fiction in new and significant ways. Godwin's *Caleb Williams*, over twenty years before Waverley, had shown the subtle encroachment of social and traditional determinants upon a man's professed beliefs. Yet the ease with which Scott grouped his characters, while still showing them as individuals, and the instinctive tact with which he refused to submerge the man in the dogma, established a high and valid standard for the novelists of what has been called " The Age of Ideology." No-one who has read widely in the fiction of the nineteenth and twentieth centuries can have avoided wishing that most of our more socially conscious writers possessed a tenth of the skill and intelligence that Scott exploited so unobtrusively.

He may still remain a problem for modern readers, however. Perhaps Alan McKillop saw it most clearly [4]: " Whole generations to come will feel the same maladjustment which Scott experienced and expressed genially, which Byron experienced and expressed misanthropically." [2] Scott's geniality is revealed in his occasionally avuncular narrative style and his customary refusal to supply the reader with any stylistic indications of a tense commitment to his task. He has no passion, complains E. M. Forster, " he only has a temperate heart and gentlemanly feelings, and an intelligent affection for the country-side; and this is not basis enough for great novels." [3] And yet in his novels revolutions occur, battles are fought, families become extinct, fanatics scream for blood,

Alan McKillop, " Sir Walter Scott in the Twentieth Century ", in Rice Institute Pamphlet, xx (1933).

E. M. Forster, *Aspects of the Novel*, p. 52.

12

CONCLUSION

" History has many cunning passages . . ."

— T. S. Eliot

In his interesting discussion of Scott and Scotland, Edwin Muir wondered if Redgauntlet's " strange cry " of defeat indicated the discovery of " an issue transcending history." [1] It is difficult to answer him, for Scott also wrote the Conclusion, which returns the reader to the conventional world with a thump. The truth, perhaps, is that Scott's quest for reconciliation and peace was perfectly genuine and that *Redgauntlet* comes closest to fulfilling it. On the other hand, such moments are difficult to sustain in the best of men, and Scott's later career as man and author exhibits the bitter triumph of necessity and his own pessimism. Even without our knowledge of his personal tragedy we would be struck by the difference between *Redgauntlet* and the Malachi Malagrowther letters. In this attack upon English financial policies Scott exhibits some power of invective, and it is perfectly obvious that John Bull is often the target, not only because he is strong, wily, commercially aggressive, and very much in the saddle, but also because he is no Scot. Nor is this Malachi's only concern, for the letters attack the impending historical changes of the Era of Reform in a way that varies from cogency to incoherence. In other words, Scott was acting the

[1] Edwin Muir, *Scott and Scotland*, p. 159.

role of one of his fictional die-hards, attacking the stranger from the future or from the other side of the border and doing so with gusto.

Yet it is in two masterpieces of short fiction that Scott, with the most disturbing objectivity, returns us to the world of harsh fact that for a moment was dissipated beside the Solway. *The Highland Widow* is the tale of a woman whose overlapping ancestral hatreds of Saxons, Lowlanders, Hanoverians, Camerons, and " progress " lead her to bring about the death by court-martial of her only son. The effect of the story is totally serious, the style has its own antique dignity, and the result is a distillation of the tragic feeling embodied in the Fergus MacIvors of the previous novels.

Even more chilling is *The Two Drovers*—a tale which yields to no major realist before or since in controlled irony and dis-abused clarity of vision. Robin Oig M'Combich and Harry Wakefield, one a Highlander, the other an Englishman, agree to travel together as they drive their cattle to a fair in the north of England. At first all goes well, partly, as Scott emphasises, be-cause Robin is an unusually cosmopolitan Highlander. But soon he drives a bargain for the rental of grazing land with an English proprietor along the way, and Wakefield, excluded from the arrangement by sheer chance, begins feeling his ancestral dislike of the northerner. His resentment is nourished at a pub by drink and the sympathetically provincial remarks of his compatriots, who have a yen for some excitement, and he challenges Robin to a fight, not for lethal ends, but for the purpose of relieving his feelings and clearing the air. But Robin's way of fighting is not the English way. He suggests the gentlemanly broadsword, with victory for the man who draws first blood. The English gather-ing laughs at such aristocratic pretensions, and here Scott's story becomes savagely ironic. A good fight, it appears, requires a common nationality! Robin becomes a lonely, badgered High-lander, aware that he is a comic victim whose honour is lightly regarded. So he blindly resorts to the method of his forefathers, and his dirk settles the argument for ever.

Sometimes it appears as though all human relationships in the

M

Waverley Novels are capable of distortion by connexions ᵛ family, clan, party, region, nation, or belief. From fanatics Burley and Claverhouse to the Bishop of Oxford in *The Fo of Nigel*, who was " equally willing to become food for fag defence of the Latinity of the university as for any article religious creed," Scott's men and women are bent b adherence, conscious or unconscious, to their factions o of life, and the outsider is always a threat. It is as Thwackum and Square had re-entered the English n armies at their backs. Small wonder that Scott four casional Cuddie Headriggs and Alick Polworths Such men do not fill drawing rooms, council chambers, fields with their frenzies.

But if Scott's characters are so often moved b political, social, ideological, or ethnic consideratio also unique individuals, and here we must acknov Scott's chief virtues. I refer to his highly realisti the way in which group loyalties vary with indiv ments. For Scott there are no totalitarian fac *Old Mortality* the intense doctrinal light of mi is refracted and coloured by the different per Scottish Covenanters. Burley's Calvinism i of Ephraim MacBriar, or Habakkuk Muckl Maclure, or Mause Headrigg. And on the oth dens differ with each other in their Toryism, the very symbol of their cause, is like a str Scott seems to have needed no apprentices conciling men and their group interests. *Waverley* describing Edward's arrest as a covers nearly a full doctrinal spectrum. fanaticism of Gifted Gilfillan, the more John Mucklewrath, the suspicious Ha Major Melville, the enlightenment of growing sentimental Jacobitism of E ranting Jacobitism of Mucklewrath's v such a *tour de force* of discrimination S to the fact that social conviction, imp

women are condemned for child-murder, acquaintances of an hour fight to the death.

We may answer Forster by pointing out that Scott's passion is in his characters, and that his handling of such scenes as Jeanie's interview with the Queen and Ravenswood's confrontation of the Ashtons shows Scott's genuine commitment to the rhetoric of fiction as he knew it. Yet he still " scribbles away about Early Christians," and there will always be those who will condemn him for criminal evasion of the demands of his subject matter.

Let us suppose, on the other hand, that his style meets the demands of his subject in ways whose strangeness to us is an indication of something we have lost. We should not regard this as impossible. For one thing, we have seen that in Scott's world men and women, trapped in the cunning passages of history, are threatened with defeat at every turn, and that for all those who meet their doom honestly—even William de la Marck—he has his measure of compassion or respect. Let us add to this awareness the realisation that Scott's humour and tolerance are not escapist gestures, but reminders that he appeals to the cosmopolitan consciousness. For all his intense feeling for locality he writes for Europe in the best and widest sense, and if we are everlastingly to play the role of Balfour of Burley or Claverhouse to his Henry Morton we are indeed in trouble. Our present duty is to seek some way out of the murderous consequences of our own fanaticisms. Whatever success we achieve will be measured according to our ability to recapture some part of Scott's catholic and humane point of view.

INDEX

in *The Two Drovers*, 18, 168. *See* SCOTLAND AND THE SCOTS.

conflict between old and new : 10 ; in *Guy Mannering*, 29, 32 ; in *The Bride of Lammermoor*, 101-105, 108 ; in *The Fortunes of Nigel*, 132-4, 137-8 ; in *St Ronan's Well*, 146-8.

contemporary and near-contemporary subjects : Scott's difficulties with, 42, 145-6.

contradictions : in Scott, 1-10, 167-168 ; in *Guy Mannering*, 31 ; in *Old Mortality*, 62, 66 ; in *A Legend of Montrose*, 116 ; in *Quentin Durward*, 124 ; in *The Fortunes of Nigel*, 129-31 ; in *Redgauntlet*, 155, 158.

Cooper, James Fenimore : 37.

cosmopolitanism : in Scott, 9, 18, 29, 171 ; in *A Legend of Montrose*, 114, 117 ; in *St Ronan's Well*, 148 ; in *The Two Drovers*, 168. *See* HUMANISM.

Crawford, Thomas : 66.

crowds and groups, Scott's handling of : in *Old Mortality*, 49-50 ; in *Rob Roy*, 71 ; in *The Heart of Midlothian*, 86, 89-90 ; in *Quentin Durward*, 122 ; in *St Ronan's Well*, 144, 147-8 ; in *Redgauntlet*, 161-2 ; reconciliation of group with individual identity, 169-70. *See* CHARACTERISATION.

Cruttwell, Patrick: 7n.

Daiches, David : 2n, 12, 79n, 95-6, 162n.

Davie, Donald : 85.

description and setting : in *Guy Mannering*, 35 ; in *The Bride of Lammermoor*, 35, 104.

Dickens, Charles : 138, 144, 154.

dogmatism and fanaticism : Scott on, 45 ; in *Old Mortality*, 49-50, 59, 65 ; in *The Heart of Midlothian*, 87-8, 91 ; in *The Bride of Lammermoor*, 102 ; 104-105 ; in *A Legend of Montrose*, 117 ; in *Redgauntlet*, 155-7 ; in *The Highland Widow*, 168.

Donizetti, Gaetano : 8.

drama, influence on Waverley Novels : 7-8 ; in *Old Mortality*, 54 ; in *The Fortunes of Nigel*, 129, 138 ; in *St Ronan's Well*, 140-1.

Dryden, John : 3, 54.

dualism : 10 ; in *Waverley*, 21 ; in *Rob Roy*, 76-7 ; in *Redgauntlet*, 151-2. *See* HEROES AND HEROINES.

Duncan, J. E. : 120n.

Edgeworth, Maria : 13, 52, 119.

Eliot, T. S. : 167.

epistolary method : in *Guy Mannering*, 33 ; in *Redgauntlet*, 150-2.

fathers and guardians : viii. Worthless fathers and guardians, 3-4 ; in *Waverley*, 13-14 ; in *Guy Mannering*, 31 ; in *The Antiquary*, 35-6 ; in *Old Mortality*, 57-8 ; in *The Heart of Midlothian* ; 87-8 ; in *The Bride of Lammermoor*, 99. Father-child relationships, viii ; in *Waverley*, 13, 21-2 ; in *Rob Roy*, 68-70, 74-5, 78 ; in *The Heart of Midlothian*, 96-7 ; in *The Fortunes of Nigel*, 133-4 ; in *Redgauntlet*, 152-5, 161. Scott's attitude toward his father, 2-4 ; reflected in *Waverley*, 22 ; in *Rob Roy*, 68-9 ; in *Redgauntlet*,